BITCH ARE YOU STUPID?

No more being used, lied to, cheated

on and wasting your time!

FORMER PLAYER

authorHOUSE

AuthorHouse™
1663 Liberty Drive
Bloomington, IN 47403
www.authorhouse.com
Phone: 833-262-8899

Published by AuthorHouse 09/14/2023

ISBN: 979-8-8230-1463-2 (sc)
ISBN: 979-8-8230-1462-5 (e)

Library of Congress Control Number: 2023917499

CONTENTS

IMPORTANT READ THIS: MOST WOMEN CAN'T HANDLE THE TRUTH BECAUSE THE TRUTH HURTS

1. You're wrong about men. These are just your opinions.
2. You can't speak for every guy.
3. All men are different. You can't say that they're all like this.
4. Your advice was way off.
5. Why's everything black and white with you?
6. Not my man!
7. You think you know everything!

These are the typical comments and responses I've received from some women who didn't want to accept my council as fact. One woman even asked what my credentials were. Well, I'm not a certified therapist, but I'm a guy. Also, the difference is, a therapist won't look you in the eye and tell you that the man you're in a relationship with isn't in love with you and you should walk away. If they did they wouldn't make any money and be out of business. It's their job to tell you what you want to hear and keep your hopes up by recommending relationship exercises and counseling rhetoric. That's how they pay for their children's college funds, by keeping you planted in your loveless relationship.

I've learned that whenever you challenge a woman and tell her anything about her man that she doesn't want to hear and make her take a closer look at her relationship/marriage; in most cases she'll become defensive. Some women want to buffet what they hear and receive. They feel, *Well I'm going to eat this, but I won't eat that. I'll accept what you're saying about this, but I won't accept what you're saying about that.* All I can tell them is, "Game is trying to give you game, you better take advantage." I've found that even if they ask me I can't always convince a woman that the man she's in love with isn't in love with her, especially if she's in a relationship with him. A woman doesn't want to hear that the man she's playing house with doesn't think of her as the core of his desire. The reason so many women around the world keep finding themselves heartbroken and disappointed is they continuously try to see things in their men that aren't there. When it comes to their man, right or wrong, some women are content with the way things are and aren't interested in peeling back that other layer to see what's underneath. That's what this book is about, seeing what's really beneath the surface of the things men do and say and sometimes the truth hurts. Some women don't want to believe or hear that when it comes to their man it's just black and white. They want to dig and find a more profound meaning when there is none, which is why some women create excuses for their man's negativity or passive-aggressive behavior. They say things like.

1. He's physically abusive toward me because he was abused as a child.
2. He's physically abusive toward me because he grew up watching his dad beat on his mom.
3. He's bipolar.
4. He's in love with me he just shows it in his own way.
5. He has a fear of intimacy because his parents abandoned him as a child and that's why he won't commit to me.

One woman even tried to convince me that the reason her man was emotionally abusive toward her was because he grew up as a gang banger in L.A., and I didn't understand the hard life and experiences that he went through. She suffers from, "He's so misunderstood" syndrome. Not only is it nonsense but the facts are these particular men aren't in love with these women, bottom line. That's why they treat them the way they do. Don't misunderstand me, I'm not suggesting that a boy who watched his dad beat on his mom won't grow up to have some psychological issues. But no matter what any therapist tries to tell you the truth is if he were in love with you he wouldn't be beating on you today. Not only is he not in love with you but he also has psychological issues that you should have walked away from a long time ago. Women today should be at a point in their lives where walking away from a man who treats them as less than is as natural as praying or brushing their teeth. However, I've found in a lot of cases that some women don't want to leave him. Sometimes women find fault with me because I'm so fast to say, "Walk away!" They don't want to walk away from a relationship that they've invested so much time and emotions. Instead, they want to stay with him and find solutions and ways to fix their "problems." Especially if there are kids involved. Then you have women who won't leave but instead want me to teach them manipulative mind tricks to make their men appreciate them more. Nope! In other cases, some women don't think there is a problem. I have many female friends who are married, and I know that their husbands aren't in love with them, but I won't tell them that unless they ask for my advice. They feel that they seem to be getting along great in their marriage and the family is all-good so why pry? Because a man playing house with you and a man being in love with you are two different things. That's what this book is teaching you. Either he loves you because you're his partner, or he's in love with you because you're the core of his desire.

Every chapter in this book won't appeal to you or have any relation to your personal experience. Some things you'll know already and be common sense, some things will be new for you, and other things you'll be in total disbelief and denial. Also, for all of you sensitive women reading this, you might not like or agree with everything I say. You might not like my tone and in some cases my smugness, but not agreeing with me doesn't make me wrong. Remember, I'm not here to mock or downplay your feelings and emotions; I'm here to help you and open your eyes.

Nevertheless, if you still decide you don't like what I've taught you after reading this book then all I can say is good luck on your journey. In the end you take on the consequences, I'm just the messenger; you don't have to take my word. Sometimes the truth hurts especially when it's not what you want to hear.

Remember, when a man is genuinely in love with you, the relationship is easy, not hard.

WHO AM I?

OK, let's cut to the chase. How can I help you and what makes me so qualified to give you advice about men? I've been a dog, that's why. I have humped more legs, sniffed more butts and buried my bone in more places than I can count. What also makes me qualified is because I'm a man, and every negative thing you can think about a man and his behavior I've been him and I've done it all to women and then some. For the record I've never physically hurt a woman, that I don't tolerate.

I have used and manipulated so many women for personal gain and my sexual, physical pleasure that it would make your head spin. The crazy part is, out of the 200+ women with whom I have had sex, I can only recall maybe ten or fifteen of their names. Seriously, that's how bad I was.

Now, on the positive side, I'm also more enlightened, sensitive and logical than the average man and because of that I'm going to pay back all the women whom I've hurt and used over the years by giving you the confidential information about the men in your lives. I'm here to answer all of your questions about your man and men in general. I'm here to tell you all the secrets about men so you don't have to waste another day with a liar, cheater, asshole or someone who's not your real soul mate. I'll tell you how men think and why they do the things that they do to women. I'll spill the beans and let you know if your man is worth keeping or if you're wasting your time. I'll tell you if he wants to be in a loving, fulfilling, committed relationship with you or not, and I'm never wrong.

For over 25 years I've counseled and helped, (meaning I've had friendly conversations with) hundreds of women from friends, associates, co-workers, strangers, black, white, young, old, married, engaged, single, mature, immature, smart women and even the hard-headed ones who can't seem to let him go no matter what he does or how bad he mistreats her. Yes, I've helped a lot of different women from different backgrounds and the one thing that all of their situations had in common whether their men were cheating, flat out wasn't in love with them or whatever the situation would be, was that I was always 100% correct. Not because I'm such a smart guy, but because I'm a man who knows how men think. Again, I've been every guy that you've ever dated and then some.

What inspired me to write this book was, one day while talking to my supervisor at work, who I always gave relationship advice to, said to me, "You know a lot about men. If you wrote a book not only would I buy it but I would tell all of my friends to buy it." That comment made a light bulb go off over my head and on that very night I went home and began typing what would turn out to be this book you're reading. The objective here is to teach you the difference between a man who loves you and a man who's in love with you. You must learn the difference because this is what will save you time and years.

Your man isn't special and no exception to the rules, and I'm here to give you brutally honest answers. Let's get started.

1

MEN AIN'T SHIT AND WE KNOW IT

What women don't know is men actually have a low opinion of themselves. It's true, we do. If you only knew how insecure, unsure, weak and scared we really are and how much we wish to be someone else it'll blow you away. Yes, I'm talking about the guy that you've convinced yourself is the greatest thing since the internet. We honestly don't feel good about ourselves and I'm not talking about his penis size, body or even financially; I'm speaking emotionally. We can't think of anything good about ourselves so we wait for you to tell us if we're great or not.

You might like a guy because he has a nice car, wears nice clothes, has a nice house, flaunts his money, etc. You think that these qualities make a man great, hot, all that. But in reality, it's the opposite. He's not great and only driving that nice car, wearing those nice clothes, buys that nice house and flaunts his money because he knows he ain't shit and it's the only way he feels that he can impress you or women in general. You show me a guy at the club with the most pimped out ride and rims and extreme sound system and I'll show you the most insecure guy at the club. The thing is women will treat that guy like he's something special and unique because his packaging comes with so much flash, in reality he's more insecure and has more of a low sense of self-worth than you do.

2

WOMEN HAVE ALL THE POWER! YOU'RE THE ONES WHO TELL US WHO WE ARE

Everything that men do in our society is designed to impress women. Our primary function is to attract the opposite sex. You're the ones who tell us what cars to buy, what clothes to wear, what our bodies should look like, what it means to be cool and sexy. You're the ones who tell us what these things are. You set the bar and the standards. We're just trying to live up to the standards that you set because we think it'll get a reaction out of you. What I'm saying is men don't put on these performances because we want to, or we enjoy acting this way. We don't want to spend our money on the material items that we buy. We do these things because in the end we think that we're going to attract a female. Possessing these material items such as cars, jewelry, nice clothes, following the latest trends/fads are our way of trying to live up to the standards and ideas of what we think women want to see.

If women told men that eating three hard-boiled eggs every day would make them more appealing to a woman, then we'll eat three hard-boiled eggs every day, believe that.

The truth is you women have all the power, and without realizing it you actually control men. But instead of using your power to control men and control the tempo of how men treat women in our society, you've allowed men to take all of your ammunition and use it against you. What do I mean? If you don't treat us like we're great or special then we have no ammunition to use against you. We as men can only use against you what you give us.

If women ever realize that they have all the power and secretly control men and exercise this information you'd be very dangerous. However, remember, knowing something and exercising it are two different things.

For the record, I'm not talking about mind games, being manipulative or giving him attitude. I'm merely talking about seeing him for what he is, not the illusion of him that you've created in your mind.

YOU WANT PROOF?

Here's an example. Mary was dating a guy named Todd, and would always treat him like he was all that and was at his beck and call. She gave him sex whenever he wanted it; always cooked for him, brought him food when he requested it. She gave him money when he asked for it and would sometimes pay his phone bill or car note. Point being, she treated him as if he was special. She did all of this while he continuously disregarded her feelings. One day she came to her senses and cut him and all of her charity off cold turkey. She wouldn't even return his calls. She was no longer at his beck and call and was no longer putting up with being treated like a second class citizen. No, this is not a story about Mary finding self-respect or standing up for herself. Moving on.

Todd did his best to put things back to where they were between Mary and him by trying different mind games, like using anger, when that didn't work he tried to be nice and sweet, promises of changing. Now, you might say that Todd was acting in all these different ways because he was lying and full of shit, and you'd be right. But there was another reason why he acted out by showing anger then sweetness. Because Todd wasn't secure in who he was to himself and in her eyes. He tried different approaches until he thought he could find one that worked and he failed, because either way she was non-responsive. You see, in the beginning, since he wasn't **emotionally evolved**, he acted out in this unappreciative, disregarding manner and she continued to respond to it. Once she was fed up and cut him off cold turkey he tried other approaches, and when that didn't work he didn't know what else to do because in the end he didn't know who he was to her or to himself. Once that power was taken away he was just a pathetic small person. You see, it's all about taking that power away from him.

3

I'll explain it in another way. Do you know the reasons why we dump, use and degrade women who are good to us? It's because, again, we don't feel that way about ourselves. In other words, *if she's treating me good, then something must be wrong with her. Why else would she be treating me as great as she does? Can't she see that I ain't shit and have so many deep-rooted insecurities and issues? If she knew that deep down I really don't know what the fuck I'm doing and I'm scared as hell of life, she wouldn't be giving me the time of day. But, since she continues to treat me good and I know I'm not as great as she thinks I am, then something must be wrong with her. She must be slow, stupid, mentally weak, or nothing special at all.*

We're so fucked up and insecure that half the time we don't even know what to do when a good woman is standing right in front of us treating us the way we want. So again we end up convincing ourselves that something is wrong with her when she's good to us. That's why we try to place value on to women who don't acknowledge us or give us the time of day, in other words, "A challenge."

PAY ATTENTION NOW CAUSE IT'S ABOUT TO GET SERIOUS! "THE CHALLENGE"

Women believe that the reason a man wants a woman who's, "a challenge," is because he thinks if he has to work for it then she means more or she has more value. Also he has a need to chase and conquer, but that's not true. Yes, in life we do appreciate something more when we have to work for it or put in our time, like a new house, car or a job, however, the reason we like a woman who's, "a challenge," is for an entirely different reason.

The truth is we're drawn to "the Challenge," because we feel that deep down they can see us for who and what we are, nothing! And they treat us as such by blowing us off or dismissing us. Why would we chase and long after a woman who we feel sees us as nothing? Because in some sick twisted way we believe that even though we still have to try and impress the "Challenge Woman" we don't have to feel insecure about ourselves because she already knows we don't measure up to her. She knows that we're weak, pathetic, lost puppies who need to be held and scratched behind the ears. In short, "we ain't shit!" Now that we know that she knows "we ain't shit" we're less game playing, bullshit and we're more sincere and vulnerable in our conversation with her. Instead of conversing with her like Rottweiler's we converse with her as wimpy puppies. She controls the leash and we let her lead. We feel that the woman who's "a challenge" has figured us out and can see us for who and what we really are. However, we feel the ones who can't see us as we really are and kiss our asses, put up with our abuse, let us mistreat and cheat on them deserve everything we do to them. Why? Because they refuse to see us for who and what we really are, and shitty abuse from us is their consequence.

Like I said it's sick and twisted. You treat us great we treat you like shit; you treat us bad we kiss your ass. Of course I'm not talking about every single situation, but I'm giving an example to women who are dealing with this type of particular man and situation.

3

I GOTTA KNOW, DO YOU THINK I'M SPECIAL?

Here are some examples, if you know a guy with a ten-inch penis you can tell him that his dick is too small and you like bigger dicks. Guess what, no matter what other women have told him about his big penis, because you said it was too small, he'll actually start to believe that he has a small penis. That's how simple it is. "He is what you say he is."

If you're in bed with a guy and he's making you scream in ecstasy and he can see that he's giving you one orgasm after another, when the sex is over, you just look at him and say, "I don't want to hurt your feelings but it wasn't all that great." Even if you know it was great guess what, he'll believe that with you he was bad in bed just because those words came out of your mouth.

If you know of a man who makes you laugh and he can visibly see you pissin all over yourself from the jokes he's telling you, after you stop laughing, you look him in the eyes and say, "You're OK, but you're not that funny." Even after he witnessed you and everyone else who's around laughing and pissin all over themselves from his humor, he'll begin to think that he's not that funny. Also, it shakes his confidence. Now, why is that? Because men respond to the negative things that are said about them a hundred times faster than the positive things said about them. That's why he is what you say he is.

Basic psychology teaches us that whatever someone says you are you'll imitate that behavior. If you walk up to a co-worker tomorrow who's always quiet and tell them that they're funny and they're really not, every time they see you that co-worker will go out of their way to be funny around you. Every time you get coffee at the convenient store and you tell the morning clerk who always seems to be grumpy how much you love his positive attitude, he'll switch up and always make it a point to be positive and upbeat when you walk in the store. He'll drop the act once you've left, but around you he'll always be cheesing; why is that? No, they're not being phony, but the reason we respond in such a manner when someone says we are something or someway is because.

1. We love positive re-assurance.
2. There's a guilty side in all of us that doesn't want to let our audience down.

It's basic psychology, but also works when you say something negative about them. If you say we're assholes, we'll act like an asshole around you. Again, if he's got a ten-inch penis but you tell him he's small he's going to believe it. We'll consciously and subconsciously become the puppet while you pull the strings. Because we know we ain't shit we're waiting for a woman to tell us what role to play and how valuable we are.

LET'S MAKE IT MORE PERSONAL

Think hard about a guy who you think is really attractive. Are you visualizing him? OK, now, let's say that he's at the club, standing at the bar, looking as good as he thinks he does. Then, one hundred women at that club walk up to him and tell him that he is fine as hell! What would happen is he would start to feel pretty good about himself, all the women want him. Then again he already knows he's the shit, right? But then the hundred women walk away, and out of nowhere one woman walks up to him and tells him that he is very unattractive, and then she walks away, leaving him feeling confused and rejected. Of course to make it look good in front of his boys he'll say something like, "Fuck that bitch, she ain't shit anyway!" But the reality is, for the rest of the night and probably the rest of the year, his thoughts and attention won't be on the one hundred women who told him that he was fine as hell, but, on the one woman who told him that he was very unattractive. Why? Again, men are more drawn and respond to the negative things that are said about them than the positive things, because deep down we believe it's true. As men, we believe we ain't shit, so we wait for you to tell us if we're something great or something repulsive. It's that simple. The point is, now she has the power over him, and he would love to spend the rest of his days trying to change her mind and get her approval and validation. See how it works?

GEORGIE BOY

There's an episode of Seinfeld where the character George was trying hard to get Jerry's new girlfriend to like him as a friend. He was extra nice to her and tried to be as funny as he could in her presence. All he wanted was to leave a good impression on her. Later, she would admit to Jerry that she didn't like George at all. When George found out about this he became obsessed and infatuated with her. It got to the point where he told Jerry that he couldn't stand the idea of her not liking him so much that he had become attracted to her. Mind you, at the same time, George already had a girlfriend who was in love with him and treated him special. However, that didn't matter, because one woman was treating him like shit. Also, the more she treated him like shit the more his fondness for her grew. So why did George respond to Jerry's girlfriend's dismissive behavior in this way? Because deep down George knew that he wasn't shit and she could see right through him. Like any man he was attracted and drawn to the woman who could read and see him for what he really was, nothing.

If you act like we're something great then we're going to believe it and either use that knowledge to take you for granted or appreciate you. If you tell us that we're something bad, we're just going to tuck our tails between our legs and put all of our focus onto you to the point where we want to give birth to your children.

The bottom line is, we ain't shit and we know it.

4

WOMEN GIVE MEN WAY TOO MUCH CREDIT

This is the number one problem when it comes to a woman who continuously lets a man disregard her feelings and lets him treat her like crap. You give men **way** too much credit. I'm telling you right here and now, we're not worth the effort. We're not that special or even one quarter as great as you make us out to be. Listen, we're just guys, people, and human beings, made out of the same materials that you are. The only difference is you have an innie and we have an outie.

Women are always creating illusions about the guys that they're with or attracted to that don't exist. The things that attract you to him whether it be sex appeal, attitude, swag, aggressiveness, confidence, aren't there at all, you've just bought into these illusions. We're elementary non-complex beings, and yet you women are continuously pulling your hair out over us by trying to figure us out. If you knew how he really was, meaning, (just a person) you wouldn't be crying over him, you wouldn't be arguing with him, you wouldn't be missing him; you wouldn't be going out of your way for him. Truth be told you probably wouldn't even be talking to him or given him the time of day. I tell you here and now if women could see men for what they really are the world would never repopulate because all men wouldn't seem attractive or worth the effort to you. By being naive to this fact you're the one who says he's special and he's all that, you're the one who validates his ego, you're the one who puts him above you, you're the one who says his way is right and your way is wrong. Guess what, he's not even worth fighting for, but you'll convince yourself he is. You women continue to put something that's beneath you above you.

Believe me, he's not who you think he is. He's nothing special and only as great and wonderful as you make him out to be in your mind, nothing more nothing less. We're just as fucked up and confused as you are if not more, but we act as if we have it all together. Yes, I'm talking about your man. Again, you give men **way** too much credit.

5

WOMEN ARE SMARTER/ STRONGER THAN MEN

It's true, women are smarter than men. Women are designed to be thinkers, analyzers, insightful, and the voice of reason. Most importantly you're more patient than we are and that automatically gives you an advantage over us. Men aren't patient. We're big babies who have to have our toys and candy right now! We want what we want when we want it. Men are also the aggressors, hostile, over reactors, act first and think later beings. However, over the years, somehow women have allowed men to make them crazy, unbalanced, unworthy, to have low self-esteem and to feel like second-class citizens. Women all over the world have allowed men to set the standards for their self-worth. As a result of that, women have taken their internal gifts and suppressed them deep inside of them until they become like a candle that was once full of wick and ready to burn and shine for the whole world to see, to being reduced to a melted blob waiting to be thrown out. Unfortunately, most females today don't even know that they are designed to be thinkers, analyzers, insightful, and the voice of reason, or that they're even smarter than men. Trust me, you are.

IF YOU DON'T BELIEVE YOU'RE SMARTER THAN MEN JUST READ YOUR BIBLE

To misquote the Bible, God may have made man in His likeness, but He made woman in His mindedness. Let me explain. Think of it this way. After Jesus rose on the third day and revealed Himself to His followers, out of all of His followers whom did He reveal Himself to first? Mary Magdalene, a woman.

Why do you suppose that He revealed Himself to a woman first as opposed to one of His male disciples? Because when all of Jesus' male followers were hiding, scared and fearful for their lives and their minds were filled with confusion and desperation, Mary Magdalene, again a woman, was calm and at peace. Even though she was sad and in mourning over the separation from her Lord, her mind was still clear and focused on Jesus' promises.

In layman's terms, she was smart enough in her thinking to handle it, and had to prepare the men for the good news because truth be told, if Jesus had revealed Himself to the men first their small minds wouldn't have been able to handle it. Even though they didn't believe her testimony, Jesus still trusted her, a woman, to plant the seed. In fact, when the men finally saw Jesus they thought He was a ghost.

Do you remember the story of Samson and Delilah? Well, here's a refresher. Samson was the strongest man in the world who wrestled lions and in wars destroyed soldiers by the thousands. All the men across the land were in awe of his remarkable strength. However, it wasn't a soldier with a razor-sharp sword or a sturdy beast that brought down the mighty Samson; it was the cleverness and cunningness of a woman, Delilah, who brought him down, which would eventually lead to his demise. She didn't even have to break a sweat. All she had to do was use her mental strengths for evil purposes, and she got what she wanted.

I'm not suggesting that you use your mental strengths for abusing men or anyone for that matter, but you're endowed with intelligence, insight, instincts and intuition that we as men don't have overall. That's what I'm talking about when I say that you're smarter than us. I'm not talking about your college education or how great you are at solving math problems or even if you can solve Wheel of Fortune puzzles faster than he can. I'm talking about the gifts that are inside of you, a women's INSIGHT, INTELLIGENCE, INSTINCTS, AND INTUITION; this is what you have over us.

Furthermore, women are more drawn to wisdom than men are. Why do you think more women attend church than men? Because women, more than men, have the insight and intuition to figure out that they want and need help and understanding from a higher intelligence and being.

6

ALL MEN ARE LITTLE BOYS

Yes, you heard me right, all men are little boys, every one of us. Your dads, uncles, boyfriends, husbands, bosses, the football/basketball players and boxers you see on TV. All the big bikers you see riding their Harley's around town, the cops and firefighters that serve and protect, the construction workers who build our houses and businesses and the men you see preaching the word of God at your local churches. We're all just little boys on the inside.

Let me ask you a question. In the beginning of the world why do you think God created Eve? Well the Bible says it's because Adam needed a helper, but helper is just a delightful word for saying babysitter. Adam was just a little boy who needed someone to help watch over him. That was until the babysitter got into the liquor cabinet, got drunk and decided to convince the child to eat the apples that were in the refrigerator drawer that had a post-it on it that said, "Don't eat the apples." But aside from that she was still the adult in the situation.

WE'VE ALWAYS NEEDED A FEMALE TO WIPE OUR NOSES AND KISS OUR BOO BOOS

From the very beginning of our male lives men were designed to want and need to reach out to a woman's love and affection. For example, when little male babies would cry out at night, we would want the attention of our mothers to comfort us. If our mother wasn't around any other woman who was soft and nurturing would do. The point is we never wanted a man to comfort or nurture us; it had to be a female.

As little boys when we fell off our bikes and scratched up our knees we didn't want our dads to kiss our boo-boos and put a band-aid on it, no, we wanted our mothers to do it. If a big bully was chasing us down the street we didn't yell out for our fathers, we yelled out for our mothers, "MOMMA! MOMMA! HELP!" What's the point I'm making? You see, since all men were born, we were designed to need and want the affections and nurturing of the female species. It's because of your nurturing nature that keeps us men as adult infants. I'm not saying that it's something you initiated or started, it's just your nurturing instincts to comfort that makes all men feel incomplete without it and dependent for your tenderness. There's no reversing it, no going backward.

WHEN HE'S IN TROUBLE WHO DOES HE REACH OUT TO FOR COMFORT?

On the surface it would appear when a woman's in trouble she has to run to a man for security, to be her hero. However, the truth is, are you ready for this? You're our heroes. We're the ones who have to come running to you when we're in our time of need. Think about it this way, no matter how much a man treats you like crap, disregards your feelings. No matter how tough he tries to act or how much of a "bad boy" he thinks he is, as soon as something traumatic or bad happens to him like a car accident, loss of job, or as soon as he gets into serious trouble with the law, like gun possession or drugs charges and is facing serious prison time, who is the first person he reaches out to for comfort, his mother, sister, wife, mistress, girlfriend, etc. That's right, a woman. We don't reach out to a man like our dads, brothers or our guy friends even if we're close to them. As grown-up little boys we're designed to need the comfort and affection of a nurturing female. Even if we treated her like crap, it doesn't matter because as soon as we're in a bad situation she becomes the best commodity in our lives for that moment.

DON'T BELIEVE ME? ASK A FORMER CONVICT

I have had so many friends and associates that did prison time, and even though each one of them did their time in different prisons and different states all of their prison stories had one thing in common. Each friend told me that no matter how big or tough the prisoners were or how brutal and vicious their crimes, and no matter how badass they acted when they were in the yard, at the end of the night when the lights went out, all you would hear were the echoes of these same tough guys lying in their beds and sobbing their eyes out like little boys. When the lights go out you can't hide from what you really are.

WHAT'S THE POINT I'M MAKING?

Stop treating men as if we're these big masculine tough guys that we're not, that turn you on whenever you feel we take charge or control. When in reality we're all just little boys. No matter what illusions you create in your mind about us this is how it really is.

Yes, I know your boyfriend beat up two guys at the same time at the bar with one hand tied behind his back, he's still a little boy. Yes, I know your boyfriend is a gang banger who participates in drive-by shootings and drug deals, he's still a little boy. Yes, I know your dad wrestled a grizzly bear and defeated it while only using a Swiss pocketknife; he's still a little boy. Yes, I know your boyfriend has a lot of cool, sexy tattoos on his muscular arms and shoulders, he's still a little boy. Yes, I know your husband started three successful businesses from the bottom up that are making a high profit, and he's an excellent provider, he's still a little boy. It doesn't matter how smart or intelligent you think he is, or if he can speak six different languages and quote Socrates and narrate the tale of Gaius Julius Caesar and the fall of the Roman Empire, he's still a weak little boy.

ARE YOU IN A RELATIONSHIP WITH MAX OR BILLY?

I see women all the time going around treating men as if they're gods and being at their beck and call. I see women trying to please these little boys and doing their best to hold onto him regardless of how bad they treat them. What you don't realize is you're trying to please and win the affections of a little boy. Moreover, the only time you should be trying to please a little boy or make him happy is when your little boy is trying to please and make you happy.

For example, imagine you're a single mom with two twin boys. One of the boys, we'll call Billy, never listened to you, never did his chores or homework, never cleaned his room, tries to come and go without telling you where he's going or when he's coming home, and never picks up his mess unless you yell at him to do these things.

Your other twin son, we'll call Max, always listens to you, always does his chores and homework, cleans his room every day, never walks out of the front door unless he has your permission. And whatever messes or spills he makes he cleans up right away and does all of these things without you ever having to tell him.

Now, I ask you, what son would you favor? Sure, you love both of your children equally and would gladly give your life for either one of them, and you want to do what's right for them. However, which one of the boys deserves a weekly allowance? Which one deserves to play video games after dinner? Which one deserves to watch an extra hour of Netflix before bedtime? What am I asking? Which guy deserves the GOODS that you have to offer? Your mind, your attention, your concern, your support, your body, your lovemaking, and last but not least, your love?

Unfortunately, we live in a world where females keep trying to give their hearts and minds to immature little boys like Billy. You see the difference is, Max might be a little boy, but he's not immature. Even though the mother loves each boy equally only one of them is causing her stress, heartache and frustration and making her life a living hell. The other boy is making things easier on her and not causing her to stress or to worry.

WOULD YOU GIVE A FIVE-YEAR-OLD THE KEYS TO YOUR CAR?

Women could save themselves from so many headaches and heartaches if they could swallow this concept and realize that the man that they're letting take them on an emotional roller coaster ride is nothing more than a little boy.

Think about it this way, if you were driving a car with a five-year-old boy in the back seat, would you stop the car and hand him the keys, scoot over and let him take control of the wheel and let him drive the car anywhere he wanted to while you sit in the passenger seat wondering where you two are going? No, I don't think you would, why? Because that would be crazy and insane. Yet, everyday millions of women are putting the brakes on their common sense and giving little boys the keys to their hearts, letting them take control of their emotions and also letting them steer them into a direction that they don't want to go into while they sit in the passenger seat wondering where this relationship is going. It's no different. I just hope that your little boy is potty trained.

IN CLOSING

It's true; we need you more than you need us. Overall, the only thing a man is really good for is sex and lifting heavy objects. Even though I say that all men are little boys they're still two types of little boys, one is a little boy, and the other is an emotionally immature little boy. Which one is your guy?

So the next time you look at your man, especially if he mistreats you, just say to yourself, "Under all of that, he's just a little boy." So stop letting that little boy give you stress, heartache and headaches. Put his ass up for adoption and walk away.

7

EITHER HE LOVES YOU OR HE'S IN LOVE WITH YOU. LEARN THE DIFFERENCE

NOTE:

This is the most critical chapter in this book because it's the foundation of what this book is all about.

PAY ATTENTION

OK, here it is. I'm going to reveal to you the ultimate truth about men in this chapter, why we miss treat you, take you for granted, disregard your feelings and why we can't give you what you need emotionally. Also, I'll explain why we're non-affectionate/romantic toward you and why we can't even be supportive in the simplest of circumstances. The answers to these questions are very simple and it all comes down to one reason and one reason only, and that reason is, "HE'S NOT IN LOVE WITH YOU," PERIOD!

That's it, that's the bottom line. This is what it all comes down to, I promise you. He treats you this way because he's not in love with you.

TRUST ME ON THIS

Look, you could save yourself from so much headache and heartache if you would take the time to learn the difference between a man who loves you and a man who's in love with you. Everything you ever wanted to know about a man and his inconsiderate unaffectionate behavior toward you all comes down to these six words.

I'll even do you one better. If you don't believe me when I tell you that the reason your man disregards you is because he isn't in love with you, then you don't even have to read the rest of this book. Return it and get your money back. Spend your money on something else more useful like putting gas in the car, toilet paper or whatever.

If you continue to read the rest of this book and absorb the knowledge I'm giving and passing onto you, exercise what I teach you in these chapters and learn the difference between a man who loves you and a man who's in love with you, then you'll save yourself from years of heartbreak and disappointments, that I can guarantee and promise you.

WHEN HE ONLY LOVES YOU

Now, don't get it confused. Just because your man isn't in love with you that doesn't mean that he still won't be kind and considerate toward you.

When your man **only loves you**, he can still be caring and respectful toward you. He'll still enjoy spending time with you and taking you out to dinners and movies. He'll spend time with your family and friends, he'll talk with you on the phone for hours, he won't say or do anything to hurt you, and he'll be good and decent toward you. You're like two best friends who are dating and can share and laugh about anything.

However, regardless of all of these positive moments you two share, either way you're still not the one who he wants to be with in a long-term committed relationship. Why? Because you're not the core of his desire, the center of his emotional thoughts. In the back of his mind he still wants to see if someone better will come along. He's waiting for someone who'll stir up that fire that's in his belly. Someone who'll make him lose sleep because he can't stop thinking about her, who'll make him jump out of the shower to answer his phone in hopes that it's her calling, who'll make him spend money he doesn't have or can't even afford. Subconsciously that's who he's waiting for, and unfortunately it's not you.

Sure, he thinks you're an awesome person, and he loves the fact that he can talk to you about anything and you two can converse on so many different levels. You're always there for him when he needs you and he likes hanging out with you. In bed he loves that trick you can do with your tongue, etc. You have so many qualities that he admires and he thinks you're great as an individual, but it doesn't matter, because again, you're not the core of his desire. The truth is you're nothing more than just something to do for right now. You're an ideal back up if maybe all else fails. In short, he **only loves you.** This is one scenario of a man who only loves you and I'll tell you many more throughout this book.

WHEN HE'S IN LOVE WITH YOU

When a man is **in love with you,** you're the center of his thoughts, the core of his desires. He can't wait to talk to you and see you. When something good or exciting happens to him he can't wait to tell you about it. He'll call you for no reason. He loves to touch your skin by holding your hand or kissing you on your cheek or neck. He'll wrap his arms around you for no reason. You can expect unexpected forms of affection and attention. He pays attention to the little things like your interests or even your favorite foods, and wanting to make you happy becomes a significant function to him. Any burdens that are on your shoulders physically or emotionally he wants to take them off you. He wants to be your hero, and he wants to be your big pillow when you fall.

Yes, when a man is in love with you you'll know and see the difference and that's what this book is all about, learning the difference between a man who loves you and a man who's in love with you. I will continuously and redundantly beat this into your brain throughout this book, and when I say walk away from him, I mean just that, WALK AWAY!

8

HE KNOWS IN THE FIRST FIVE MINUTES OF MEETING YOU IF HE WANTS YOU

In the 1980's TV show, Married With Children, there was an episode where the character, Bud Bundy was trying to impress a girl by acting like a bad boy extremist and doing activities like sky diving and river rafting. All of these activities he was participating in were designed with the hopes that his bad-boy persona would make this girl want to have sex with him.

His older sister, Kelly, got tired of watching her brother make an ass of himself, sat him down and told him the truth according to women. She said, "Bud, it doesn't matter what you say or do for a woman, or how much you try to impress her. A woman knows when she first meets a guy whether or not she's going to sleep with him. If she hasn't slept with you already, then she doesn't want to."

Now, I'm not a woman, so I don't know if this is true from a woman's perspective, but, I'll say that from a man's perspective the same principles do apply.

HE ALREADY KNOWS WHERE YOU'RE GOING TO STAND WITH HIM

Most of you out there didn't even know this about men, but yes, it is true, a man knows within the first five minutes of meeting you where you're going to stand with him. He's already sized you up in his mind. Whether it is conscious or subconscious he already knows what part he wants you to play in his life, if at all.

A man knows in the first five minutes if he wants to be in a serious relationship with you. He knows if he wants you to be the core of his desire, only wants to date you casually, only wants to use you for sex, only wants to be your friend, only wants to be your friend with benefits. He knows if you're just going to be a booty call, going to blow you off, cares whether or not he might hurt your feelings, can see himself marrying you, can see himself falling in love with you, or if he can see himself dating you because it could be convenient for his present situation, etc.

The majority of women don't even know this information about men so they waste so much of their time trying to hold onto a man who's disregarding their feelings or mistreating them, thinking he'll change his ways or eventually come around and appreciate the woman he has. Nothing could be further from the truth. In the first five minutes of meeting you, he already locked you into what position you're going to play in his life, and whatever positions he's put you in, good or bad, nine times out of ten, he won't see you in any other way. So, if he's disregarding your feelings or mistreating you in any way, it's because he's not in love with you and knew from the beginning, again conscious or subconscious, that he was never going to be in love with you. Stop wasting your time and walk away!

9

IN THE BEGINNING, IF HE'S TALKING ABOUT OR PRESSURING YOU FOR SEX

When a man meets a woman who he's interested in and the courting phase has begun sex is the last thing on his mind. He doesn't care about it, he's not anticipating it, and he'll have the attitude of, *it'll happen when it happens.* He's not going to do anything that ruins his chances of being with her and that includes pressuring her for sex. He's just going to wait and enjoy spending time and getting to know her. He's content with just a gentle kiss after dinner or when she allows him to hold her hand during the movie. Believe it or not, these little token signs of affection from her means more to him in the beginning than her spreading her legs for him. It's not that he enjoys the chase or looks at her as a challenge, but what it does is it makes him appreciate her even more and builds up excitement and anticipation, and that pedal stool that he's put her on gets higher and higher.

I just spoke about how, "A man knows in the first five minutes of meeting you if he wants to be with you," so believe it or not, some guys, when they feel that they've met "the one," actually prefer not to have sex with her too soon, because they don't want to taint the image they have of her. So having said that, when a guy meets a woman and he can already see his unborn children in her eyes or other words "Wifey," he'll automatically put her in a different category in his mind. It's the, "She's special" category. That means she's unique, hard to find and not a dime a dozen. So initially he'll approach and treat her as such. He'll build her up to be something great and different. Usually, it's because she's pretty or has a pretty smile, has a beautiful body or aura, and if her conversation is positive, confident and sincere it's the icing on the cake and he'll become gaga over her. For now that's the image of her that he wants to keep.

Now, don't misunderstand me, in your case, yes, he's physically attracted to you, yes, he wants your body, yes, he wants to put his hands all over you and feel on your breast and ass. Yes, he's looking forward to being inside of you and climaxing, but at the same time he's not going to pressure you for sex if he genuinely wants to be with you. In his mind he's too concerned with just trying to seal the deal and keep your attention and make you his woman, period! Working on that plan is hard enough, so the idea of trying to get you into bed is out of the question because that's just more unnecessary work and a headache he doesn't need.

10

DOES HE KEEP BRINGING UP SEX WHEN YOU TALK ON THE PHONE?

You ever find yourself talking to a guy on the phone who you don't know that well and he keeps gradually trying to lead the conversation into sex but you don't want to talk about sex? Yea, you quickly pick up on it and keep your answers short then try to change the subject, but he keeps trying.

As guys, we know when a woman isn't interested in talking about sex. We try not to be too obvious about it, but women know what we're doing. When I knew that my attempts to initiate sexual conversations with a woman on the phone weren't working I would try to be slick. I would lie and say something like I just saw a condom commercial on TV and then ask the woman what types of condoms she liked or felt good to her. I would pretend that I saw a bra commercial on TV and start talking about bra's in constructive ways so I could slowly bring the topic around to her breast, while at the same time acting nonchalant about it. Sometimes it worked and sometimes it didn't; either way these weren't women I was in a relationship with and I wasn't planning on ever being with them. Bottom line, if he likes you he's not going to try and initiate sexual phone conversations.

Now, if he hears you talking about anything sexual he might try and add to the conversation to see where it might lead, but the keyword is lead. He'll let you lead and not rock the boat. When he hears that you're trying to change the subject he'll follow. He's not stupid, and he knows when to shut up.

Trust me he's not even going to hint about sex or passively bring it up. He has bigger things on his mind, like making you wifey. He wants it to work so much that even when you bring it up he's still going to play it cool, why? because he wants to be with you. However, if a guy you don't know that well keeps trying to throw sexual content in the middle of the phone conversation, then pretend you went through a tunnel and hang up.

DOES HE ONLY CALL/TEXT YOU AT NIGHT?

Something else to look out for is when he only seems to call or text at night. He's not picking you up to take you out to a nice dinner. He's not going out of his way to impress you. He only seems to text or call you at night to see "wats up?" The obvious answer is, his dick.

11

SEND ME SOME PICTURES

If a man truly wants to be with you and he's still in the, "Trying to impress/get to know you phase," he's not going to ask you to text him any sexual pictures of yourself. I can't stress this enough. When a man who you haven't given the green light to, and especially hasn't proven himself to you, asks you to text him some dirty photos of yourself, is a **MAJOR** red flag. Why? What that means is not only does he not have any plans on ever being with you, but it also means that "you ain't shit!" to him.

As guys, when we ask for naked pictures from a woman who we know that we haven't proven ourselves, shown any affection or sincerity to, that's because we don't plan to, and she's disposable to us. We hold her in the same regard as a used condom on the floor. **We wouldn't be asking for naked photos from a woman whom we're sincerely trying to court and get to know.** Because if we like you we respect you, and again we're not blowing any chance we have to be with you by asking or hinting for something as your tits on our screen saver. We have all the time in the world to see you naked and to ask for naked pictures, but for right now, we want to win your heart.

DON'T TAKE THE INITIATIVE BY SENDING HIM NAKED PHOTOS OF YOURSELF

I've had women who I liked and was trying to get to know send me naked photos of themselves too early without me having to hint or ask for them. Now, did it kill my attraction for them or make me stop pursuing them? Not necessarily.

But it can bring you down a few pegs in a guy's mind. It sends a loud signal of insecurity. It makes a guy wonder why you feel the need to initiate and send naked photos of yourself so early on. He'll think maybe you're not as unique as he thought, and if you are willing to send him some pictures in the beginning without him even asking for them, how many other guys are walking around with naked photos of you?

You might think taking the initiative by sending him dirty photos of you might help secure the deal and enhance his attraction for you. But, it can easily have the opposite effect and take you from the, "She's special zone," to the, "booty call zone."

12

WHY DO GUYS LIKE TO SEND ME DICK PICS?

Yes, a lot of men like to send women pictures of their junk. Just know off the top that any man sending you a sexually explicit picture too soon is not serious about getting to know you, wanting to be with you or even has any respect for you, especially if you didn't ask for it.

There are a few reasons why men do this, but let's create a scenario first. You meet a guy at the bar. He seems nice, decent and someone you wouldn't mind maybe going out or sleeping with in the near future. And then that same evening he texts you a picture of his junk? WTF?

Why did he do that? Easy, because he sees you as an easy target. He's not that attracted to you and thinks that you're probably grateful that he's even acknowledging you. So he has no problem with doing something so bold and direct. He thinks that he has nothing to lose by jumping into the deep end head first. And if your response isn't a positive one, well then it's no loss to him, because after all, he wasn't feeling you that much to begin with anyway.

LOOK HOW BIG I AM!

If a man is well endowed he believes that his chances are better and you'll get turned on once you see his size. After all, he's used to women wanting to hook up with him because of his endowment, and sending texts of his junk to women whom he has just met in the past might have worked well for him but some women such as yourself get turned off from it.

Another reason why some guys can be so bold in texting you pictures of their junk is because big men get a thrill when they see women getting excited about their size; it makes them feel desired, wanted, in control like a sexual beast that women want. It's an ego boost.

Guys like revealing their freaky side especially if they think or believe that a woman is open-minded enough to handle it. And sometimes on first impressions a woman can have a strong essence of sexual energy and can seem so sexually open-minded and cool that a guy thinks that she'll be OK with him sending her a dirty picture of himself. He thinks that she'll respond with a message that says "Nice!" or "Very tempting!" Sometimes a woman is impressed and likes what she sees and responds with a text of validation. But, if he doesn't get the response he wants he'll get the message that she's just turned off and not interested at all and move on. At least most guys will move on.

IN CLOSING

You're obviously not the kind of woman who responds to these types of advances. I'm sorry that these particular guys always attempt to make you their target for their freaky exploits. And like a lot of women, until you meet Mr. Right you'll probably have to endure and expect this type of unwanted, unappealing behavior from men you have encounters with from time to time, because unfortunately they don't come with signs on their shirts that read, "I'm a freak and I'm going to send you a picture of my dick!"

13

HOW COME GUYS CHANGE AFTER THEY HAVE SEX WITH YOU FOR THE FIRST TIME?

Guys change up after having sex with you for two reasons.

1. They weren't that serious about you in the first place.
2. They lose respect for you for sleeping with someone like them. Remember what I said in the chapter, "Men ain't shit and we know it?"

However, when a man knows deep down that he's not planning on being in a long term relationship with you, once he gets that orgasm, then his real, "I don't give a shit," attitude comes out.

Women usually think the reason men act like that is because they gave it up too soon or he would have respected you more if you would have only made him wait. But that's not always true. Yes, you should make a man wait before you give him sex, but his bad attitude isn't because you gave it up too soon; it's because, again, he wasn't serious about you in the first place.

SOMETIMES IT'S JUST BECAUSE YOU'VE BEEN HUMANIZED. IT HAPPENS

There's another reason why men change after having slept with a woman they're gaga over. It's because now that the sex is over and he's got his orgasm, you've been humanized!

When we're gaga and about to have sex with you for the first time, sometimes we can't even get it up. We're panicking because we're anxious. Physically we want to more than anything, but mentally we know that we're going to tarnish the image we have of you in our mind. In other words, we know that after we have sex with you, you'll become humanized.

Before we have sex with you we think you're great, a gift, and an angel from the heavens. But when the sex begins all of a sudden the feathers on your wings begin to fall off. Subconsciously we start to take you off that cloud and bring you down to earth. All of a sudden we'll start to see you as a person and not as this perfect woman. Now that you're naked we can see your stretch marks and your breasts aren't as perky as they looked when you were wearing that red shirt. Your vagina has a little odor to it, not a bad one but we can smell a little something is there. After the sex is over and you're lying next to each other, we can smell that your breath isn't as fresh as it could be. It's not a bad thing, but some of your flaws that we didn't notice before because of our blind infatuation start to reveal themselves. But don't worry it's just a temporary reaction.

Because we're gaga over you, we'll begin to put you back on that cloud again and continue to treat you like the angel you are. However, if he doesn't come back to his senses and continues his asshole attitude I highly recommend dropping his ass today.

14

YOU'RE JUST SOMETHING TO DO FOR RIGHT NOW

That's right; all my female friends out there with low self-esteem, you're just something to do for right now.

Every day millions of women allow themselves to get put into this category by men to be, "Just something to do for right now." What does this mean? He has no plans on ever being in a loving, fulfilling committed relationship with you. He feels you're not worthy, you're not good enough, and you don't measure up. You don't have "the right stuff." You're not what he wants in a potential mate. You're just convenient for the time being. He doesn't know exactly what he wants but what he does know is you ain't it!

Long short is, you're just something to do for right now.

Now, he's OK with hanging out with you, dating and even moving in together, but to be blunt all you are to him is someone to fill the void until something better comes along, or he gets tired of you, whichever comes first. Ten times out of ten if a man has already put you into this category he's never going to want you romantically.

THAT DOESN'T MEAN HE WON'T BE GOOD TO YOU

A man can be totally nice, good, and even respectful toward you, but regardless, he'll still put you in the category of just being something to do for right now.

Just because a man doesn't think that you're good enough for him to want to be in a relationship with, that doesn't necessarily mean that he doesn't care about you or would want to see any harm come to you. It just means that you're not what he wants as his love interest. In most cases the reason is that he's not physically attracted to you so he'll hang in there with you until something better comes along. Of course there can be other reasons, but the physical reason would be the main one. Stop allowing men to place you in this category and acting like naive little girls trying to convince yourselves that in time he'll learn to appreciate you romantically because it ain't gonna happen!

MAYBE HE IS AN ASSHOLE TO YOU

Another no brainer, if he's continuously an asshole, unappreciative and inconsiderate, then either way it's not good for you regardless of what category you fall under in his eyes. You're still just something to do for right now.

WHAT I TEACH YOU IN THIS BOOK
FALLS UNDER THIS CHAPTER

I could have easily called this book, "You're just something to do for right now." The majority of the stuff that I speak of in this book falls under this category. If a man is not treating you the way he should be according to the teachings and standards of this book then he's not in love with you, and you're just something to do for right now. Walk away!

15

MEN AREN'T AFRAID OF COMMITMENT

OK, grab a chair and scoot up close to me because I'll need your undivided attention. Turn your TV's and phones off and if you have long hair tie it into a ponytail so that it's not covering your ears. Can you hear me now? OK, here it goes, MEN ARE NOT AFRAID OF COMMITMENT! YA GOT THAT!

In the history of humankind this has never been true. A man being afraid of commitment doesn't exist. The idea that men are afraid of commitment was probably created by some woman who wrote for Cosmopolitan magazine years ago to validate the reasons why the man in her life wouldn't commit to her.

My answer to this myth is nothing new. When a man says he's afraid of commitment, what he's really saying is, he doesn't want to be committed to you! Bottom line, he doesn't find you that attractive, you don't really do it for him and he could probably do a lot better if he's patient. You're sweet, fun to hang out with and he enjoys watching movies with you. Oh yeah, and the sex is cool.

The thing is he would never tell you how he really feels about you because he would never want to hurt your feelings. So, when a man says he's afraid of commitment or has trust issues, trust your instincts not to commit any more of your time. Walk away!

16

MEN AREN'T AFRAID OF BEING HURT AGAIN

Don't ever believe a man when he says he can't commit to you because he's afraid of being hurt. Technically to some degree everybody is afraid of being hurt by someone that they have feelings for, or they love. Regardless of how many times a man's been hurt it won't stop him from pursuing a relationship with someone he's currently attracted to or has developed feelings for. If he says he's afraid of being hurt, it's just his nice way of saying he doesn't want to be in a serious, committed relationship with you! The same rules that, "Men aren't afraid of commitment," also apply here.

Truth be told, when a man has been hurt and we've had a couple of weeks of mourning and boo hoo-ing, what we want more than anything is for another woman to give us attention and to validate us once again, especially if we're attracted to her.

The reason we want another female to give us attention is because we're still hurting. Think about it this way, when a man has crashed his car that he really loved and washed every other day, it doesn't mean that he doesn't want to drive again, it means his motives are to regroup and get another car even better than the first one. And this time instead of washing it every other day he'll wash it every day. As men we don't have time to be walking or catching the bus or bumming rides from friends; we want a vehicle that we can call our own, to polish and fill the tank up every day. If a salesman is trying to give us a great deal on a new car with a fresh start, then there's no way in hell we're going to turn it down. But, having said that, it also doesn't mean that you're the one who can feel that void, because the fact that he's hurt over her means he really loved her. So it could take a particular type of woman to bring him out of his funk. It just might not be you.

SOMETIMES DATING A GUY WHO'S RECENTLY BEEN HURT ISN'T A SMART IDEA

Sometimes, after a man has been hurt or dumped by his woman, he'll have a hard time letting go of her emotionally. He may genuinely actually like you and have feelings for you, but he's still harboring feelings and thoughts for his ex. His heart won't let someone else in just yet until it knows that there's no chance for him and his ex to reconcile. Unfortunately, sometimes it can take years for him to get her out of his mind and system. In his mind he'll be thinking he might be able to make it work out with her, or they might get back together again if he's just patient and waits. In this case, he's actually not trying to hurt you, even though he will in the end. What this means is you're just his subconscious back up. Sometimes it's not easy to know if you're his back up in this case, because a man can be using you subconsciously to validate himself and not to be alone. However, at the same time, he can treat you like a queen and shower you with attention. All this remarkable attention he'll shower you with is affection he really wants to give to his ex, but you'll do for now.

So be warned, sometimes when it comes to dating a guy who has just recently been hurt, date at your own risk!

17

IS HIS ATTITUDE USUALLY NEGATIVE?

It's human nature to build ourselves up by putting others down; I've done it numerous times myself. I used to be a Mr. Know It All, was always answering a question nobody was asking and commenting and criticizing everything like movies and restaurants, etc. As people we sometimes have to give the ones we love grace to be that way, unless they're like that all the time.

Some people in my life have given me grace; others were just plain turned off and distanced themselves from me. I asked a girl I used to date why she stopped calling me and she said, "Because you're way too critical." I still acted as if she was the one with the problem and not me. Deep down, I knew she was right, but a man who's critical and judgmental tries to see everyone else as having the problem, not himself.

HE KNOWS WHAT HE'S DOING

Your man knows that he's critical and judgmental. He knows that it's a part of his personality. Also, he's aware that it turns off the people around him, his associates, friends and especially his woman. However, the truth is, he's not in love with you. Here's why. You see, when a man is in love with a woman his love for her automatically makes him feel more positive. It changes his outlook and the way he feels inside. It's impossible for a man not to feel positive or have a different outlook on life when he's in love and has a great loving woman by his side. By instinct and nature he'll want to become a better person. That doesn't mean that he'll be walking around with a smile on his face 24/7 and not have bad days, that's not what I'm saying here. I'm saying that a man's love for his woman will add another dimension to his emotions and in turn make him a more positive and loving person. Everything about our emotions is a give and take.

Yes, there will come a time in your relationship where your man will be critical, judgmental and have a bad attitude. Sometimes he'll treat people as if they're beneath him because that's what makes us human. But in your case, if he were in love with you, he would quickly check himself and his bad attitude so as not to turn you off or push you away. Trust me when I say he knows it's a turnoff.

The plain facts are he's been this way since you met him and probably way before then. Since he continues to be this way that means you're not the core of his desire.

IT'S A REFLECTION OF HOW WE FEEL ABOUT OURSELVES

If he's critical and judgmental to that degree then he has some unresolved internal issues, that's a fact. He has a poor sense of self-worth, esteem, and being this way gives him a false sense of validation. Someone caused him pain at some point in his life and by him lashing out by being so critical and judgmental toward others is how he deals with it.

Whatever his issues might be don't entertain it and don't make it your problem, especially if he's not trying to get help or counseling to deal with his issues. Walk away.

18

DON'T BE HIS DUMP STATION

What do I mean by dump station? I'm talking about the guy who constantly bitches and complains to his woman and always makes his problems and lousy attitude the focal point of the conversations. There's a big difference between a man sharing his problems with you and dumping his problems on you. The man who shares his problems with you is in love with you, and the man who constantly whines and dumps his problems on you isn't in love with you.

Now, when two people are in a relationship it's perfectly normal for one or the other to share their thoughts about the bad day that they've had, like if someone pissed them off at work or if their just stressed out about money and bills, etc. But, if you're in a relationship with a man who's always talking about or dumping his problems on you, and at the same time he makes no attempt to brighten your day or shows any concern about what's on your mind or any problems you might be dealing with then there's your red flag.

WE DON'T WANT TO TURN YOU OFF

When a man's in love with you he's still going to bitch and complain from time to time, but he's also smart enough to know that you as his loving woman doesn't want to be his dump station or always want to listen to his bitching 24/7. Men know that it's a turn off for a woman to have to listen to a man complaining all the time, so he'll find more constructive ways to share his problems with you so as not to tire you out or turn you off with them. We as men know that a woman wants her man to be able to open up and share his day and feelings with her even if they're bad. However, he also knows that she wants a **"man"** to share his thoughts and not a whining little boy.

HE DOESN'T CARE

He's dumping his problems on you because he doesn't care about how you look at him or even if you look at him like a whining little bitch!

When a man is in love with you he wants you to see him as in control, on top of things, not easily shaken and he'll do his best to make sure you see him this way. He wants to be your hero, and a hero can't be seen as someone full of uncertainty.

A man knows he can't keep up the masquerade of acting as if he's in control forever, but he's going to do his best to try. The fact that he doesn't even make an effort means he doesn't care about how you view him or even if his whining turns you off. He's still going to continue acting this way until you walk away!

19

HE WON'T MOVE IN WITH YOU

The reason he won't move in with you is because your relationship is not that serious to him and he doesn't see a future with you. In short, you're not the core of his desire.

If he can't see himself waking up next to you ten years from now then he's definitely not interested in sharing a bathroom with you. Why should he give up his independence and be tied down to someone who doesn't do it for him in that special way? Think about it, he has to leave his options open, and moving in with you closes that optional door just a little bit more. In his mind you're just his girlfriend not his soul mate. You're just something to do for right now, but not later. He'll also give you every excuse under the sun as to why he can't move in with you and do his best to make them sound logical, but it's all bullshit.

IF HE WERE IN LOVE WITH YOU HE WOULD JUMP AT THE CHANCE

Remember, a man in love can't wait to move in and share a space with you. What moving in together signifies to a man in love is he's one step closer to sealing the deal, because the next step is marriage. You see, marriage is his ultimate goal, and whatever steps he has to take to get that much closer to walking down the aisle with you he'll do it.

Don't get me wrong, I'm not saying that moving in together is some chess game to a man where he's always plotting his next move, not at all. He wants to move in with you because he's in love with you and wants to start a life together. But if you're supposedly in a relationship and he won't move in with you, then he's not in love with you. Walk away!

BE CAREFUL. HE MIGHT NOT BE IN LOVE, BUT JUST USING YOU

Sometimes a man needs a place to stay because he's not doing well financially. So, he'll move in or get a place with his girlfriend out of convenience. In his mind it's just temporary until he gets back on his feet financially. Sure, he doesn't have his own space anymore but he'll still be cool with it because after all, she's there to cook, clean and give up the ass when he wants it. Plus, part of the financial burden is taken off his shoulders. If he's not treating you according to the standards that I set in this book then you'll know the difference.

20

DOES HE ROUTINELY ASK YOU FOR MONEY?

Many women, who are dating a man, usually make the mistake of continuously giving him money. Now, if you're in a real, honest, trustworthy relationship and he has a real financial problem or is involved in a rare financial circumstance, then of course, there's nothing wrong with helping or being there financially for your man.

For instance, let's say he was laid off from his job because business is slow, and he has a car note coming up in two weeks that he might not have enough to cover, that would be considered a valid financial circumstance, and of course it's OK to loan him the money. If he gets a call that one of his family members who lives in another state was in a car accident and is in the hospital in critical condition and he's a little short and needs to borrow a few hundred dollars to buy a plane ticket, again, that's considered an unfortunate circumstance and it's OK to loan him the money. If he calls you out of the blue to borrow fifty dollars and doesn't even offer an explanation as to what the money is for, again it's OK to loan him the money. Let's say he does lose his job and while he's out of work for a month or two you help him out by buying him groceries, paying for his cable or electric bill, and in the meantime he's going out on job interviews and is making an effort to find work, that's OK too, because he's making the sincere effort to straighten out his financial situation and you're just a supportive, loving girlfriend. That's a good thing.

The real problem is when he has a job and still continuously asks you for money. Or if he doesn't have a job and makes no real effort to be employed and is continuously asking you for money for trivial things like to put gas in his car, cigarettes or to pay his phone bill. Or he asks you to buy him items like shoes or clothing, etc.

CAN'T BUY ME LOVE

Unfortunately, most women make the mistake of thinking that being there for their man when he continuously asks for help, especially in the financial department, is a good thing, that makes them a good woman, and her man will appreciate that she has his back when he needs her, WRONG! She also feels if she doesn't continuously give him money or buys things for him when he asks, he'll stop calling and coming around her, RIGHT!

If you have to give him money or buy him things because you think money equals love, then what you don't realize is he was never yours.

KIA

I had a friend named Kia. She called me one night to borrow two hundred dollars. She told me she needed it to bail some guy out of jail, "Wait, back up?" I said. "Who is this guy? And what's happening?" She told me she met a guy a few nights before at the club. They "really hit it off." So on this night he got pulled over. They took him in for warrants. He called her up to see if she'd bail him out. What was sad was she was anxious to do it too. So me, being the know it all that I am, I explained to her that she needed to leave this punk alone. I told her, "He just met you two days ago, and he's already asking you for money to bail him out of jail? First of all, if he really liked you, he wouldn't be calling you from jail or letting you know he got locked up. Second, he definitely wouldn't be trying to borrow money from you and asking you to bail him out." Because as guys when we're in the courting phase we always want to make a great impression, look good in your eyes. But of course she wouldn't listen. Instead she got defensive and said, "forget it, I'll get the money another way!"

In her mind, because she liked this guy/stranger so much, she felt that if she showed him that she would be there for him and have his back when it counted that he in return would appreciate her more, and eventually he'd be her man. Well, guess what? She bailed him out, and she never heard from him again.

HE'S NOT IN LOVE WITH YOU

He has no problem continuously asking you for money because he's not IN LOVE or CARES or RESPECTS you, period!

The truth is, no man that's genuinely in love with you is going to ask you for money repeatedly. The reason he won't continuously ask you for money is that he would want you to see him as a man who can provide for himself and also take care of you in the hopeful near future when you two eventually move in together and get married.

When that time comes, when he has to legitimately ask you for money because a circumstance arose, whether it is significant or trivial, he'll feel a little embarrassed and ashamed to have to ask you for it. He doesn't want you to think of him as less of a man. That's usually just his insecurities running away with him, but it's true, he'll feel like he's not doing his job if he has to ask you for money or a loan. Since he doesn't like that feeling he'll try to avoid asking you for financial help. Keep in mind; he'll only feel ashamed if he's genuinely in love with you and is serious about taking the relationship to a higher level.

IT'S OK. I LOVE MY MAN. I LIKE BEING THERE FOR HIM WHEN HE NEEDS MY HELP

That's not the point. Remember, it has nothing to do with how you feel about it. It's about how a man in love feels about himself having to ask his woman for money and wanting to be a provider. Yes, a man in love will have to ask his woman for money from time to time, but in his mind he should still be the provider for his woman, and he acts on it. It doesn't matter how much money you make at your job or even if you make more than him, he still wants to be a good man and take care of you. No, I'm not talking about him being controlling, holding the finances over your head, or wanting you in a position to have to ask him for money so he can keep close tabs on you. I'm saying a man in love wants to do right by his woman and relationship period!

Remember, when a man is in love, he always feels a little insecure to some degree and he knows if he doesn't do his job you might go out and find someone else that will. So if he's continuously asking you for money, walk away!

21

RAISING, BABYSITTING, PROVIDING FOR AND TAKING CARE OF A GROWN MAN?

There was a time in American society where it was understood that the man was the breadwinner, the head of the household. It didn't matter what your background was, men took pride in taking care of their families. They went out and dug ditches, laid train tracks, worked overtime in the cold and heat depending on what part of the country they lived in, and even walked long miles to get to work. They did this because men understood at that time that a man takes care of his family, period! Even if they were poor men, they were the hardest working poor men that you would ever meet. Somewhere between then and now something in our society has changed dramatically. Men in our modern-day society have become mentally weaker and lazier. A lot of men don't want to work, take control or have responsibilities and show no motivation about doing anything or setting personal goals for their lives. In other words, lazy ass, video game playing, couch lounging, channel surfing, texting about nothing, running up the food and the electric bill, no good for nothing parasites. However, this is also a two-sided coin because many women in our society have become enablers to these so-called immature dumbasses. Yes, so as much as this makes him a lazy dumbass, this makes you an even bigger dumbass for entertaining it, Ms. Enabler. It's accountability time.

What's wrong with your self-esteem where you would let some man live up in your house or apartment and he isn't even trying to be a provider for you? I mean hell, you already did the hard part, you put the roof over both of your heads.

IF HE LOVED YOU, HE WOULD WANT TO PROVIDE FOR YOU

So, let's get down to business. This man living in your house isn't in love with you. I'll make some of the same points that I made in the, "Does he routinely ask you for money?" chapter.

When a man is really in love with you he's naturally going to do his part as a man to be a provider and take care of you and the household. He wants to provide for you, he wants to do for you, and he wants to make a home with you. Even if it's a simple apartment, a man in love wants a loving woman to come home to and a positive environment. If he's not doing that then the bottom line is he's not in love with you and doesn't respect you.

Remember, when we're in love we want to do our part and be a good, responsible man, so you don't get turned off and possibly leave us for someone who can provide better for you.

HE'S BEEN TRYING TO FIND A JOB

The real question you need to ask yourself is, *Why am I taking care of and providing for this grown man?* If he says he can't find a job he wants he's full of shit. Don't get me wrong, I've been in positions where I struggled with the job market, but I still did what I had to do. The truth is if this man were in love with you, which he isn't, he would go out and get two temporary jobs at McDonald's and Taco Bell if that's what it takes to pay bills and be a good provider. You see, it's not just about him physically working a job, even if he does go out and gets a job that's not the real issue. The point is, if this man were in love with you, from the beginning he would have automatically taken the initiative to do what's right for his woman and his relationship. He wouldn't have even let it get to that point of being dependent on you. The reason it got to that point is because he's not in love with you, never was and he's just lounging around your house as a place of convenience. This guy has no goals, no ambition, and is immature. Guess what? In your naive way you decided to make it your problem. Well, you got it.

I STILL LOVE HIM

Now, let's say instead of doing the right thing and pushing his ass out on the street, you decide to do the, "I'm still trying to hold on to him because I love him," thing. You start an argument about him not working or contributing and the result is he decides to get a little job to quote-unquote "help out." Fine, but guess what? That still doesn't mean that he's in love or wants to be in a fulfilling relationship with you. It just means that, again, where he lives at with you is convenient, and if all he has to do to shut you up is get a little job and help out with the bills and groceries then he'll do it.

I LIKE TAKING CARE OF HIM

I've heard women say this, "But I like taking care of him." I know there is such a thing as women who want to feel useful in a relationship, but, this isn't the way to do it. No real man wants a woman to take care of him or provide for him, especially if he's in love with her.

IT'S OK IF YOU'RE SPLITTING THE BILLS

Don't get me wrong. Yes, a real man in love wants to provide for you, but, he's OK with equally splitting the bills with you. He just doesn't want you to have to take on more of the financial burden, if he can help it. He only wants to look like a winner/hero/provider in your eyes.

The choice is yours. If you decide to lower your expectations and hold on to him because you think this is the best you can do, then good luck raising a grown man who isn't in love or respects you.

22

IF HE'S NOT SAYING, "I LOVE YOU"

When a man is in love with his woman he loves to say the words "I love you," regularly and for no reason. He'll say it when you're leaving his presence. He'll say it while you're in the shower and he's brushing his teeth. He'll yell it out to you for no reason while you're in another room. He'll text it to you while he's on his lunch break or while he's holding you. He'll even interrupt you while you're in the middle of a sentence to softly say, "I love you." However he does it he wants to say it.

HIS REASONS ARE SELFISH, BUT SINCERE

A man who is in love always wants to express himself to his woman and say the words "I love you." It's not just because he wants to reassure his woman of his love for her or to make her feel good, and that's not meant to be selfish, but men also say it because it's a need and it makes them feel good. What do I mean? He says it because he wants to hear you say it back to him. Yes, it makes him feel good and connected to you when he says those words, but sometimes a man wants reassurance by receiving a positive reaction from you, meaning your smile, a hug or a kiss.

Whatever his reasons for saying it he means it, and there are emotions and feelings behind it. So, if he's not saying it to you regularly without you having to say it first, it's because he's not in love with you.

23

IF HE'S NOT GIVING YOU
PHYSICAL AFFECTION

When I say physical affection, I'm not talking about sexual affection. I'm talking about little everyday tokens of physical affection. Remember, a man in love always wants to touch you and looks for any excuse to touch you in some way shape or form. Your skin automatically becomes a magnet to his lips and hands. Again, I'm speaking non- sexually. Yes, there's a time and place for that too.

EXAMPLE:

He'll always want to hold your hand, walk up behind you, put his arms around you and kiss the back of your neck. He'll want to kiss you goodbye when he leaves your presence, no tongue, he just wants to feel his lips on yours or your cheek. When you're sitting on the recliner, he'll sit next to you on the floor and begin to massage your feet. If you're lying on the couch, he'll sit at the end of the couch, put your feet on his lap and rub them. When you're out at a restaurant having dinner together, he'll put his arm around you and slowly rub his two middle fingers up and down your arm or rub the back of your neck. Like I said, any excuse to touch you.

PUBLIC FORMS OF AFFECTION

If he won't give you public forms of affection or says he doesn't like to give public forms of affection then he's not in love with you. A man in love doesn't care where he's at when it comes to giving his woman affection; he just knows he wants to touch her. In most cases, he'll begin to give you physical affection subconsciously because wanting to touch you has become so natural to him, even in public.

WE HAVE TO TOUCH YOU

As men, we need the warmth we get from touching our woman's skin. Weirdly, it gives us an emotional push and we feel incomplete without it. For example, what do you do when your phone starts to lose its charge? You connect the charger to the phone so electricity can flow through it to recharge it so it can function throughout the day. Well, the same principles apply here with a man touching you. It might sound silly, but touching you recharges us emotionally and gives us the energy we need to keep going forward in our day. We have to touch you, period!

NO, I'M NOT TALKING ABOUT PEST BEHAVIOR

Don't get me wrong, I'm not saying that a man in love always wants to be up under you and smother you continually; that's not what's happening here. It just means that in his mind he feels fortunate and appreciates what he has, and these are a few examples of how a man in love expresses himself to you. Remember, when your man is in love with you he'll be magnetized to your skin. So if he's not touching you then that means he's not magnetized to your heart.

24

IF HE DOESN'T CALL OR TEXT YOU THROUGHOUT HIS DAY

If your man's not calling or communicating with you throughout his day then he's not in love with you. For any man, the highlight of his day is when he gets to communicate with his heart's desire.

Don't misunderstand me, I'm not talking about lovey-dovey bug a boo phone calls throughout the day, I'm talking about a man's basic need to communicate with the woman he loves. Yes, it is a need.

In the chapter (If He's Not Giving You Physical Affection,) I said, "We have to touch the woman we're in love with because in a weird way it gives us the emotional push to keep us going forward in our day, and we fill incomplete without it." Well, the same principles apply here. Instead of touching you we have to call you. We have to hear your voice. We feel secure in knowing that our hearts desire is just a phone call/text away. We want to share a little bit of our day with you, even if you live together and he knows he's going to see you in a few hours, it doesn't matter because he still wants to communicate with his love. If something funny or bad happened at work or on the way home we want to share it with you. Maybe we got a break in our day, so we use that time to call or send a text. We just need some form of contact with our woman to make our day better, even if it's already going good.

WE'RE NEVER TO BUSY TO CALL

We're never too busy to call or text you, believe that. What do I mean? It doesn't matter what's consuming us, we'll find a way to communicate even if it's just a quick text to say, "Hey babe, working overtime tonight, won't be able to see you until tomorrow afternoon. I love you." Also, "I know I'm running late. Let's catch the 8 o'clock movie instead of the 6:30, because I won't make it in time. Miss you." That's how a man in love communicates with his woman. Why? The last thing he wants to do is leave her hanging. He wants to give his woman reassurance just like he needs reassurance. So as much as he can he'll give her the security and reassurance that he's always considering her feelings. So much so, that a man in love begins to do it subconsciously. Trust me, if he's not calling/texting you throughout his day, he's not in love with you. Walk away!

NOW DON'T GET IT CONFUSED

I'm not saying that just because your man calls you a lot throughout the day that he's in love with you. Your man can have absolutely no feelings for you, be cheating on you and still call you a lot, believe me I used to do it all the time. I'm just merely stating that if you're in a relationship and he's not calling or communicating with you regularly throughout his day, then that means he's for sure not in love with you.

25

YOU CALL AND HE DOESN'T ANSWER

Yes, I know that women have accepted all of the excuses from their men as to why they don't answer their phones when they call them such as:

1. He's working too many hours.
2. He lost or forgot his phone.
3. His phone wasn't charged.
4. He didn't hear it ring.
5. He was at a club or bar and the music was too loud, and again, he didn't hear it ring.
6. He was talking to someone important on the other line, like his mother, or boss, that's why he didn't answer.
7. He was sleeping or in the shower when you called.
8. While driving, he thought he spotted Tupac Shukar's killer and was too busy to answer the phone because he was trying to tail the suspect in his car, but the suspect lost him on the freeway. Then, his phone fell out the drivers' side window as he was calling the police, and the excuses go on and on.

HE ONLY WANTS TO TALK TO YOU WHEN HE HAS TO

Well, guess what? It's all bullshit! Now, I'm realistic, and I understand that situations can occur and your man at some point will be involved with one of these unfortunate life-altering circumstances where he just can't answer the phone when you call him. I mean shit, I've even been involved in all of these myself, except the Tupac situation. The problem is, when you continuously have to deal with his excuses for not answering or something always seems to happen or come up when you call him.

Seriously, it's a phone not a video game. It doesn't take a NASA scientist to figure it out. The device is non-complex and straightforward, it rings we answer, duh. If we get a text and we see it comes from our woman we text our woman back right away.

So, if you're having trouble with your man not answering your calls regularly, it's because he doesn't want to hear your voice and doesn't want to hear what you have to say. You're not the highlight of his day. His day would go a lot smoother by not communicating with you too much until he has to. When he sees it's you calling he rolls his eyes and he says, "Damn, what the fuck does she want now?" When he finally calls you back he's talking in short one-word sentences or acts as if he doesn't have answers at that time, "I don't know, I'll have to see, yea, I know, I will, OK, I already did," and so on. He'll act as if you're inconveniencing him, he's bothered by having to talk to you, or he'd rather be doing something else. Sometimes he'll talk nice but he'll be rolling his eyes at the same time.

MY MAN SAYS HE DOESN'T LIKE TO TALK ON THE PHONE

This man says bullshit! Look, naive females, it doesn't work that way. Your man is no exception to the rules. The hell if a man doesn't like to talk on the phone with the woman he loves. What's happening here is your man doesn't want to talk on the phone with you.

YES, HE HAS A LIFE OUTSIDE OF RESPONDING TO YOU

Of course I'm not talking about your man being at your beck and call 24 hours a day. After all he does have his own life and circumstances to deal with daily, and yes there are times where he can't answer the phone or text you back right away, that's all of us. I know this, a man in love is always checking his messages throughout his day to see if you called or text him. Yes, there are times when I can't get back to my woman right away, but when I do finally call or text her and my response is late I'll explain myself. As a man in love I'm going to give her real answers and a real timeline about when she can expect me. Not because she's a demanding control freak who wants to know my whereabouts, or because I'm some spineless punk of a man who has to answer to his woman. It's because she's my heart, I don't want her to worry or give any negative thoughts a chance to creep into her mind about what's happened to me or what I might be doing. Who knows, she might not even be thinking anything is wrong, but guess what? I'm still going to explain myself. If your man isn't doing this then walk away!

26

HE DOESN'T BUY ME GIFTS
DURING THE HOLIDAYS

I know your man very well; Mr. "I wasn't raised to buy gifts on the holidays." He's so unique, so one of a kind, and the rules that the rest of society follows to buy our loved ones gifts on the holidays doesn't apply to him.

Unless he was raised by wolves and lived in a cave while growing up it's all bullshit. I too was raised in a family that didn't celebrate the holidays regularly, but I still know how to buy the woman I'm in love with a gift on those special occasions. Even if I wasn't in love with a woman and only liked her I would still buy her something and give her a small token of my affections.

The bottom line is your man is not in love with you. It's that simple. Again, men are not stupid when it comes to this. We know that the holidays, gifts and tokens of appreciation to express our love to our lady are essential to a woman, even if a woman acts like it isn't important.

Some women are so used to not receiving anything or some small feeble gift that they don't expect much and are happy with whatever they get, and that's sad.

WHEN HE ISN'T IN LOVE WITH YOU

Do you want a sign that your man isn't in love with you but only loves you? When Valentine's Day comes around, and your man only buys you candy or flowers. When it's your birthday and he only buys you something that he knows you wouldn't love, just like, like a new bathrobe or charger for your phone. These are the red flag gifts.

IT'S NOT ABOUT WHAT YOU WANT, BUT WHAT WE THINK YOU'RE WORTH TO US

This is what it comes down to; a man in love looks for any excuse to do something special for you, something that took some thought or a little time on his part. I'm not saying he has to do something extravagant to prove himself to you, but a man who's in love makes an effort. He'll ask female friends and co-workers their advice and input. He'll look online for hours just to get inspired and to get ideas. He'll call your mother/sisters or best friends and ask them questions about what's on your mind or what you might like. He'll also pay attention to all of the words that come out of your mouth, especially when you're watching TV. If you say you like something you saw on a TV commercial or if a woman on your favorite TV show has a particular purse that you just verbally praised out loud, when you're not looking he'll write it down or take a mental note.

You have to remember; when a man is genuinely in love with you he always feels lucky to be with you and feels if he's not on top of his game he could run the risk of losing you to a well better candidate. As well as he should be scared, after all, you're a smart, intelligent hotty!

Now, I know there are women out there who say, "I don't want no well thought out gifts, it's the little things that count and matter to me, like keeping the gas tank full or bringing me lunch at work." Don't get me wrong, those are great things coming from a man, but again, it's not about what you want; it's about what we think you're worth to us. If he's not doing those well, thought out and I can't wait to surprise her gifts, then you're not worth much to him, and he's not in love with you. Walk away!

27

HE'LL MOVE TO ANOTHER CITY OR STATE TO BE WITH YOU, IF HE'S IN LOVE

Maybe you were already living in separate cities when you met him or maybe you live in the same city but your job or a family emergency requires you to relocate to a different city. Regardless of the circumstances if a man is really in love with you and wants to be with you he'll relocate to whatever city you're living in to be with you. He has already made up his mind that you're who he wants to be with so he's not about to let you go to another city without him.

VALID REASONS FOR HIM NOT MOVING TO ANOTHER STATE TO BE WITH YOU

1. If he can't arrange for his children to come with him or get proper visitation rights. After all, a man's kids have to come first.
2. If he's military and they won't allow it.
3. If he has serious medical issues and he won't be able to get the proper treatment he needs in the new city or state.
4. He comes from a small town and that town is getting its first Wal-Mart and he wants to be there for the grand opening.

These are just some to name a few. Maybe not 4.

THE INSECURE JEALOUS FACTOR

To him, what you living in another state without him represents is, *she's in a new environment, and it's exciting but scary at the same time. She's lonely for friends and one on one conversation with another person that she can connect with emotionally. Emailing, the phone and texting are not the same. And then one day while she's at the grocery store buying Ramen noodles, she gets approached by Mr. 'His dick is bigger than my man's.' And since she's so vulnerable from the move and being a new fish in a big pond she'll respond to his advances and agree to go out with him. He'll give her the best sex that she's ever had in her life, and she'll also find out that he makes 1.3 million a year and has a fat house up in the hills.*

This is just how your man's imagination will run away with him if you're too far away. It might sound funny to you but it's real to him. It's not that he thinks that you want to cheat on him when you're away, but at the same time he knows that you're still human with vulnerabilities and can succumb to the same temptations as any woman can. Of course he can't have that.

HE WANTS TO BE WHERE YOU'RE AT

Initially, like any man would, he'll try to persuade you into not going or try to see if there is another option for you to stay, but if the result is you have to go, then you have to go.

When he's in love with you, especially if you haven't tied the knot yet, being in your presence is all that's important to him. It won't matter if he has to start over, relocate to a new city and take a pay cut at a new job. It doesn't matter if he has to sell off most of his possessions or even his car and house. It doesn't matter if it's something that he doesn't even want to do. As long as he gets to be with you, that's all that matters to him. If shipping off to a new city or state and rearranging his life around is what it takes then he's on board. Remember, he's in love with you, so his main goal is to walk down the aisle with you as fast as he can by any means necessary.

28

HE WANTS TO MARRY YOU AND FAST!

A man's goal, when it comes to the woman he's in love with, is to ultimately walk down the aisle and marry her as fast as he can to make their relationship official. He can't wait to take this step, because in his mind if you're married to him that means you'll belong to him. Now, don't misunderstand me, I'm not saying that you'll be his property or he thinks he's going to control you, but, what I mean when I say that "You'll belong to him," is he'll feel you're giving him the permanent deed to your heart and emotions. In the end that's what a man in love wants, is to have you emotionally. By you marrying him it means that in his mind he's the only man that you desire or want to be with, you've forsaken every other man or options you've had and have chosen him above the rest. Because he's in love with you he has to make this wedding happen ASAP!

HE'S GIVING YOU EXCUSES WHY HE CAN'T, IT JUST MEANS HE DOESN'T WANT TO

Again, when a man is in love he can't wait to marry his heart's desire and make it official. You won't have to hint or ask him questions like, "Where is our relationship going?" or, "Where do we stand?" because he'll beat you to the punch with a wedding ring. Trust me, when a man's in love he can't wait to pop the question and let all the other men out there know that you belong to him. But, if he's giving you excuses, stalling and trying to validate the reasons why he can't marry you at this point in his life, then it just means he doesn't want to.

HE CAN'T RIGHT NOW BECAUSE HIS
FINANCIAL SITUATION ISN'T GOOD

In the history of humanity, no man has ever looked at a woman who stole his heart and had the green light to marry her but turned the idea down because his financial situation wasn't right. A man being broke and a man being in love are two different things.

Yes, a man in love wants to be a provider and to take care of his woman, but, what women have to understand is by him being in love and getting the chance to marry you, his "heart's desire," only motivates him to want to get his financial situation straight. With his woman by his side there's no stopping him! There's no way he's going to let you slip away or let another man slide in and steal you from him in the meantime. Money or no money, in his mind he's going to marry you, and he can work out the financial situation later.

HE JUST GOT OUT OF A BAD MARRIAGE AND
ISN'T READY TO BE MARRIED AGAIN

It doesn't matter if he's been married seven times and all of his ex-wives were ax murderers who tried to kill him. If a man is truly in love, he won't hesitate to make you number eight and try marriage all over again. Do not let this man use his past marriage as an excuse as to why he won't marry you, because it's all bullshit!

Think of it like this, let's say your rich Uncle Harry dies and in his will leaves you ten million dollars, but after taxes, legal fees and expenses, you only end up with two million dollars. Yes, you would feel cheated and screwed over like you were taken advantage of, but two million dollars is still better than nothing. Now, let's say a year later, your rich Aunt Mabel dies and left you eight million dollars in her will, I ask you, just because you got the short end of the stick with the first will, will you let that stop you from pursuing the eight million dollars promised in the second will? The answer is no, because you're not about to let something with that much value slip through your fingers. The same principles apply when a man has another chance to marry somebody special. He's not going to let his bad experience from his first marriage destroy any chance of happiness he could have in his second or even third marriage. Besides, when a man is in love, he doesn't dwell on his past, with you, he only sees his future.

HE FEELS YOU'RE BOTH RUSHING THE RELATIONSHIP

That's a joke! Remember what I said, that a man knows in the first five minutes of meeting you where you're going to stand with him. What you have to understand is he already made up his mind long before the idea of marriage even entered your head on whether or not you were someone he wanted to fall in love with and marry. Bottom line is a man in love can't walk down the aisle with you fast enough! Only a man who isn't in love says that you're rushing him or giving him unwanted pressure. That's his subtle way of saying he cares about you and loves you as a person, but you're not worth marrying, and when he decides he wants to be married, it won't be with you. Don't believe any of his excuses because in the end that's what they are, excuses.

HE SAYS IT'S JUST A PIECE OF PAPER AND IT DOESN'T MEAN ANYTHING

He's right, it is just a piece of paper. However, yes, it does mean something. It symbolizes his commitment and unending love for you. If a man ever tells you, "It's just a piece of paper that doesn't mean anything," again, that's his subtle way of saying, "I'm not in love with you, but we can still chill together."

Do not walk away from him, run from him!

29

WHY DO MEN MARRY WOMEN THEY'RE NOT IN LOVE WITH?

Here are the sad answers to this question.

1. It's just something to do for right now.
2. Sometimes a man won't be satisfied with his life, so he'll get married to his girlfriend to try and fill some of the voids he feels are inside of him.
3. He'll convince himself that getting married might be what he needs to bring a sense of stability and balance back into his life.
4. He'll also marry her because it's convenient or out of obligation because she's been loyal to him.
5. He'll marry her because it's expected from their family and friends.
6. He'll marry her because it's financially beneficial to him.
7. He'll marry her because she keeps nagging him to do it.
8. He'll marry her so he can control her.
9. He'll even marry his woman out of jealousy and to keep her from being with another man.

Again, marriage is just something to do for most men who aren't in love. To a woman, it's the event of a lifetime, the beginning of a new journey together. To a man not in love, it means someone to hang out with full time until it gets old. Yes, when some men get married they don't think it's going to last a lifetime. Subconsciously, a man is thinking, we're *just going to live together until it's time to move on.*

JERRY MAGUIRE

Remember the movie Jerry Maguire with Tom Cruise and Renee Zellweger? Well, in this movie, Tom's character, Jerry, had just lost his job and had broken up with his girlfriend. He was hitting an unexpected low point in his life.

Renee's character, Dorothy, who worked for Jerry's former employers, began taking a shine to Jerry, and in short, took this down in the dumps man into her home. She also took pity and nurtured him. What did she do? In short, she entertained him. She was beginning to fall for him hard! Now, he wasn't giving her any real reason to fall for him, what I mean is, he didn't shower her with attention or express any real romantic feelings toward her. He wasn't calling her every three hours to say, "Hey honey, I'm calling to let you know that I'm thinking about you, I just wanted to say I love you." In short, he did nothing at all, but sleep with her. He wasn't even in love with her. That's OK, because from Dorothy's perspective she had enough love inside of her to carry both of them through the relationship. Stay with me now.

So, eventually they ended up getting married. Why did Jerry marry this beautiful, nice woman, if he wasn't even in love with her or showering her with romance? The answer to that is easy. He was hitting a low point in his life and had lost his job and woman. He needed to get some structure and security back into his world, so he attached himself to the only person naive enough to entertain his pathetic rock bottom self. Sure, he wasn't in love with her, but if he married her, some of those voids and potholes would start to fill up again and he would get some balance back into his life. Again, it was OK that he wasn't in love with her because Dorothy felt that she had enough love inside of her to carry them both through the relationship, right? In the end, that didn't matter, because Jerry couldn't be that loving, supportive husband that she needed and she wasn't being satisfied emotionally. She began to realize this and had to make a choice, and she made the right one, to walk away.

The problem with a man who only loves his wife but who is not in love with her is he'll eventually start to reveal himself and Dorothy was fortunate and smart enough to see the writing on the wall early on and walk away. Remember, Jerry was good and caring toward her, he never abused her physically or verbally, but that didn't matter because he wasn't in love with her, that's what mattered in the end.

Instead of him standing on a mountaintop with his sword high in the air and declaring his love for his woman by shouting it out for the whole world to hear, Dorothy found herself in a position of having to crawl up the mountain all by herself, with luggage on her back (child), just so she could declare her love for her man by shouting it out for the whole world to hear for the both of them.

Now, we all remember the scene when he went to her house and busted into the women's meeting. She said the famous line at the end and everyone had a good cry. Well, that's a movie script. The chances of your husband running back to you and wanting another chance will happen more than likely. The chances of your husband running back to you because he wants to be in a committed, fulfilling marriage with you is not likely at all.

30

WHY MEN DATE MARRIED WOMEN

If a man is attracted to a woman, the fact that she's married usually won't discourage his decision to date or have an affair with her. Yes, some men take the high road and not get involved with a married woman, but then you have those who don't care one way or the other. He'll try not to think about the wrong decision he's making. But if he has any conscious at all, in the back of his mind he knows that she's married and traded vows with a man under the sight of God, family and friends, and he knows that they share a house and have kids together. He also knows that if her husband ever found out about it, aside from wanting to kill him, it would also probably devastate him. Still, he's very attracted to her and the fact that she keeps giving him the green light he can't resist. Most guys won't even attempt to approach a married woman unless she does give him the green light or even some kind of hint that she's interested in him.

Most guys aren't exactly looking for a married woman, sometimes they'll just find themselves in a situation where they're attracted to a woman who happens to be married, like a co-worker, a woman who goes to the same gym as he does or someone who he interacts with on the regular. However, it's usually not intentional.

IT'S OK BECAUSE HER HUSBAND DOESN'T TREAT HER GOOD

Usually a woman tells the man she's having an affair with her and her husband aren't getting along; she's in a bad marriage or he's doing her wrong and cheating on her. Based on her testimony, negative home life and circumstances he'll convince himself because of that dating her is OK. *Yes, she's married and has a family, but her husband doesn't treat her good and not only do I treat her better, but we like and care about each other.* A man believes you when you tell him that your husband isn't treating you right. Not so much because he believes that you're such an honest and forthcoming woman, but it's what he wants to believe. He'll believe just about anything from your lips if it helps him squash that little voice inside of him telling him that sleeping with you is wrong.

WHAT DOES HE THINK OF A WOMAN WHO CHEATS ON HER HUSBAND

Again, many women are usually making themselves out to be the victim in their "Bad marriage." In some cases, it might very well be true. However, because he is so attracted to you and though you're cheating on your husband with him, he still doesn't see you in a negative light or as an adulterous. Instead, he sees you as a great, sweet, attractive and loving woman who's just in an unfortunate bad situation/marriage. He loves playing the part of secret hero, and he loves being the one who brings balance into your love life by not only satisfying you sexually but also being a good friend and shoulder to cry on when you need someone to come to. Even though you're cheating on your husband with him as opposed to just ending your bad marriage, he still thinks the world of you.

BECAUSE HE LIKES YOU HE'S OK WITH YOU USING HIM

This is especially true even if he sees no signs of you leaving your husband or "Bad marriage" any time soon. Regardless of the negative things that you're saying about your husband, he believes deep down that you're still probably in love with your husband. And even though you love the cheating sex and are attracted to him, you only care about him as a friend, and in the end you're just using him, but none of that really matters to him. All he wants is for you to leave your husband and start a new relationship with him, so he sincerely works overtime in trying to prove that he is the better man for you. So he feels as long as he pays his dues with you that eventually you'll come around and choose him in the end.

IT'S A CHALLENGE

For some guys it's not just being attracted to a woman who's married, but being attracted to a woman because she's married. It's less to do with her but more with being attracted to her married status and validating his ego. Of course there's something very appealing about forbidden fruit, and if a married woman is beautiful and gives him just the smallest hint or a friendly smile then he's going to want to see if he can pull her over to the dark side, especially if he's frequently around her, co-worker or whatever. It becomes a game to him, a challenge to see if he has what it takes to get her.

It's even more of a challenge when the woman shows no real sign of leaving her "Bad marriage" any time soon. But for the sake of discussion, if she does want to leave her husband and wants to get more serious with the man she's cheating with chances are he's not going to want to be with her because again, to him it's just a game. If he's physically attracted to her, then he'll keep her around before officially dumping her because now that he's won the game the appeal to play the game is gone.

SOMETIMES HE JUST DOESN'T CARE

Sometimes it doesn't matter what her situation is or if it's wrong, he knows that if a woman is willing to sleep with him then he's going to oblige. Whether she's married or not, it's all the same to him. In other words, all he sees is a vagina wearing high heels. It's easy to find guys who have minimal moral values when it comes to respecting the vows and institution of marriage. That's also a two-way street because many women don't respect the institution of marriage and are sleeping with married men as well. In this day and age married women cheat as much as men do, and because of that, as long as the woman acts like she's OK with it then he won't put up any resistance. Married or not, it's just another hole to him.

31

DATING A MARRIED MAN

QUESTION:

My name is ????, I'm writing you from Seattle, W.A. I'm currently in a relationship with a married man. I work for a cell phone carrier and he was a regular customer that would come in every month to pay his bill. Every time he'd come in we'd talk for a while and then one day out of the blue he called me at work and asked me out. We dated heavy for two months until I found out that he was married. I found out because one day after talking to him on the phone he thought he had hung up but he didn't, and I could hear him in the background talking to his friend about his wife. When I confronted him about this he apologized for not telling me that he was married, but, he said that they were separated and just living under the same roof for now for financial reasons.

He said that they grew apart a few years ago and are now just friends. He also says they sleep in two different bedrooms. He told me that they're going to get a divorce when the house was paid off and then they were going to sell it. Until then he's stuck in this position. I decided to believe him and continued dating him. I do love him, the sex is fantastic, but still everything is hush-hush. When she calls him I have to be quiet when they talk. Once, he even got mad at me when I attempted to leave a hickey on his neck. He says it's because even though they're separated he doesn't want to offend her.

Of course I have never met her or been to his house, he usually comes to my house or we meet up somewhere. Either way it's been a year and a half. I'm beginning to feel like the other woman. I love him and want it to work, but is he taking me for a ride?

ANSWER:

Flight is more like it. Let me say this can sometimes be a gray area. I don't condone a woman being involved with a married man or vice versa under any circumstances because of the symbolism behind marriage, regardless if the two married parties involved agreed to be friends and temporarily split the bills out of convenience. Being involved with someone who's married always seems to attract bad karma no matter how you slice it. Is it possible for a man to be married on paper but be separated from his wife emotionally and fall in love with someone else? Absolutely. Is that what's happening here? No.

This guy reminds me of my friends who cheat on their wives, but, let's get back to the point. So, you like this guy, the sex is good and you want this relationship to work. I want you to understand something Seattle, this man is never going to be in love with you, and you might foolishly date him for the next five years, but emotionally he'll never be yours.

IF HE REALLY LOVED YOU, THEN EVERYTHING WOULD BE OUT IN THE OPEN

If he is telling the truth about his living situation with his, "Wife," who he's no longer emotionally attached to, then that still doesn't change the fact that he isn't serious about being in a loving, committed relationship with you. You're just something to do for right now.

If this guy were serious about being with you and his marriage only existed on paper then he would have made plans to be living with you a long time ago, especially after a year and a half. If he and his "wife" are so chummy now, then he would have brought you over at least once to introduce you to her. There would be nothing to hide. Instead, he has to come over to your house and have you meet him at other locations. If he were that serious about you, he would have done everything in his power to ease your mind of any doubts or insecurities and not come across so secretive. He would have told his "wife on paper" that he's with you now and the two of them need to speed up this divorce process so he can move on with his new love and they can work out the financial situation later. Even if he was trying to be sensitive to his wife, he could still do it without alienating you and making her feel awkward, especially if they have that much of an understanding, right?

The bottom line is, you are the other woman, and I hope the sex is that good for you because in the end that's what you're selling yourself out for. Remember, if he were really in love with you, his main concern would be to make you happy and to do whatever it takes to give you peace of mind in your relationship. Walk away!

32

ARE WE BETTER OFF AS FRIENDS?

For starters, let me say that you're not better off as friends, because this guy never was your friend to begin with and never will be. He's not interested in getting to know you on a more profound friendship level, come on work with me?

Let's forget about the fact that you two have dated and even slept together for a moment. If he really cares about you and even respects you as a person or a friend he wouldn't have treated you with the inconsideration and given you the emotional abuse that he has been from the beginning. Even if he knew in the beginning that deep down in the long run he wasn't going to want to be in a relationship with you, if he cared about you and had any respect for you he still would have treated you as a person with feelings.

He is just being a guy, a guy who doesn't give a fuck about anybody but himself. Then again, maybe that's why you say you love him and want to keep him in your life because he acts as if he doesn't give a shit. Some females can't help but be drawn to a guy who treats them like crap and acts like he doesn't care.

His hot and cold attitude toward you is a red flag, and it seems he has given you every red flag in the book, but yet you've decided to become color blind.

I would like to know where your self-esteem is. He doesn't call you for days, stands you up, made it clear that he wants to sleep with other girls. and when he sees you on a date with another guy after not having called you in awhile, he decides to check in with you. That means he temporarily got jealous from seeing you with another guy and even though he doesn't want you, he wants to keep you off the playing field for anybody else. Does any of this sound like the foundation for friendship, marriage or even love? If you decide to pursue a friendship with this guy and because you're so weak, eventually he'll pull you back to where he wants you, and the next thing you know you're back in his bed. Then you'll be spending your days full of heartache and wondering why he isn't calling you again.

Let's be honest this isn't about friendship is it? The truth is you want to continue to keep him in your life in the hopes that in time he'll eventually come around. When you think he'll be ready to settle down, you'll be there waiting with your low self-esteem and open arms.

I've met your type before, and I know that you're a very nice girl with a big naive heart. That's why no matter what advice I give to you about walking away you're still going to pursue this dysfunctional relationship, if that's what you want to call it. Listen to me, he doesn't want to be your friend, he is someone that was only supposed to be in your life for a season, and now that season is over. Move on!

33

A MAN WHO LOVES HIS MARRIAGE AND A MAN WHO'S IN LOVE WITH HIS WIFE

I'll use the old series, The Sopranos, to make this next point. If you're familiar with the show then you remember the Tony Soprano character.

Tony loved his family dearly. He loved his two spoiled kids and wife very much. He bought his wife anything she wanted from fur coats, jewelry and a million-dollar house. However, no matter how much he loved his wife and marriage that didn't stop him from banging a different chick almost every other episode and having mistresses on the side. Yes, he loved his wife and even wanted her to be happy, but that's as far as his feelings and emotions went, he just loved his marriage and his wife, but he wasn't in love with his wife. What was happening here? She wasn't his love interest or desire; she was just someone to set up shop with.

Yes, a man will play house with you, split the bills and go to your parents' house for Sunday dinners and even get engaged and marry you, but that doesn't mean his heart's with you. I have many guy friends who have good wives at home but they're still running around lifting their leg on every fire hydrant they can find and coming home with a smile on their faces. No, there's nothing wrong with their wives; they're just not in love with them. Some men love playing house and love to have their cake and eat it too. They also love to have the security of a home life and a separate place to release themselves sexually.

Remember, a smart cheater keeps his dirty life away from his home life because a smart cheater knows better than to shit where he sleeps. Some wives say,

"It's OK that he cheats, as long as I don't find out about it," duh? OK, and this statement shows just how little some women think of themselves, very sad.

OK, WELL WHO CARES IF HE'S NOT IN LOVE WITH ME. WE KNOW EACH OTHER WELL AND ENJOY EACH OTHER'S COMPANY, AND WE CAN LAUGH AND TALK ABOUT ANYTHING. WE'RE PAST ALL THAT MUSHY STUFF, AND WE HAVE A DEEPER UNDERSTANDING. BESIDES, I DON'T HAVE IT IN ME TO PURSUE ANOTHER RELATIONSHIP AND I DON'T WANT TO BE ALONE AGAIN

Awesome, I won't discourage you from that, especially from a woman who can be honest with herself. However, there's a significant hole in your logic, and that hole is, now he only appreciates you, but as soon as something better comes along you're **outta there anyway!** You'll be alone again. Better to kill a bee now before it stings you. By the way, a man in love never gets tired of the mushy stuff.

HE'LL NEVER FALL IN LOVE WITH YOU, BUT HE'LL APPRECIATE YOU

Yes, he'll appreciate you, but if you think being appreciated is all you're worth then you should be content with a friendly pat on the head whenever you do something that pleases him. Yeah, that should satisfy you emotionally. He'll appreciate you when you make his favorite dish or get that stain out of his work shirt. I'm sure he'll also appreciate his dog when it takes a shit outside on the front lawn instead of the living room carpet. Do I even have to say walk away?

34

I'M FIGHTING FOR MY MARRIAGE

Listen, you can fight for your marriage until you're blue in the face, it doesn't matter. Either he wants to be in a loving, fulfilling marriage with you or he doesn't.

I understand that marriage is supposed to be a sacred thing between a man and a woman; you took an oath before God, your family, friends and you believe it's all worth fighting for. All that sounds good, but the reality is a man isn't supposed to be in love with his marriage, he's supposed to be in love with you. A man isn't supposed to be fighting for his marriage, he's supposed to be fighting for you, his woman, the person, the individual, the core of his desire. There's a reason why he isn't fighting for you, and that reason is he isn't in love with you, which means you shouldn't be fighting for him because it's an on-going fight that you can't win. The bottom line is he doesn't want you.

Thousands of women have fought for their marriages and have succeeded in keeping their marriages together. However, in the end, these women got exactly what they fought for, a marriage and a husband. Sure, he doesn't satisfy you emotionally, you're not the core of his desire and he doesn't attempt to brighten your day, but that's OK, because at least you got him to stay and live under the same roof as you, right? You have to ask yourself, is this all you think you deserve in a marriage, just someone to share space with?

So remember, if you find yourself in a position of having to fight for your marriage, then it's already over for him, at least on an emotional level. There's nothing else you can do except pick up what's left of your self-respect and walk away!

35

HAVING HIS BABY WON'T MAKE HIM STAY OR WANT TO BE WITH YOU

Many females had to learn this the hard way. Believing that if a man gets them pregnant, whether it was intentional or entrapment, that it'll make him have a change of heart, want to be with them and start a family. **Listen very carefully;** getting impregnated by him does not equal an emotional attachment from him to you. It just means that he ejaculated in you and now you have the next nine months to argue and stress over him and be given the run around while having your calls and text messages ignored. I have hard-headed female friends who didn't learn this until four and six pregnancy's later.

A guy is not thinking, *Well, now that she's having my baby, all of a sudden I feel all sorts of new feelings and emotions awakening inside of me for her. I realize I'm in love with her and want to honor her, stand by her side, do the right thing, put a ring on it, and build a home and a life with her and our child.* Can you hear the fantasy music playing in the background?

To a woman, getting pregnant represents a new beginning. It means her emotions, hormones and life are going to change. A million thoughts race through her head. It's a scary but wonderful time. To a man who's not in love or emotionally attached to you, it represents a burden, an eighteen-year burden.

Stop trying to convince yourself that if you allow or entrap him into getting you pregnant that he'll come around emotionally and want to be with you. If he wants to be with you he'll be with you, and a fatter belly isn't going to determine his mindset or emotions one way or the other. The reality is nine times out of ten it's the opposite effect, and he'll only be in his baby's life as much as he has to or can be, or walk away from both of you all together. Even if he's supportive throughout the pregnancy and plays an active role in the child's life that'll be great, but he's still not going to be yours.

Either way it's a house of cards waiting to fall because his emotions are still a million miles away. Remember, when a man truly wants to be with you it'll be from his heart and not what's in your stomach.

36

BABY'S DADDY

Unfortunately, women are always allowing themselves to get pregnant by immature un-evolved dumb asses, sad, but true. After they let an idiot impregnate them they want the right to complain about his uncaring non-involved attitude.

Well, guess what? It's accountability time. Let's take a look at some of the classic complaints.

1. He doesn't visit his son.
2. He's only seen his baby girl three times and she's already fourteen months old.
3. He never gives me money.
4. He gives me money, but he never spends any time with his child.
5. He's only bought three boxes of diapers since his son was born six months ago.
6. He never even came to the hospital when his daughter was born.
7. His son doesn't even call him daddy.
8. He only calls his son when he's locked up in prison, but when he gets out we never hear from him.
9. He never wants to talk to or asks about his child, but he always wants to talk about him and me getting back together.
10. He doesn't do anything for the baby or me, but we still sleep together from time to time.

Most of you women need to stop because you knew exactly how he was before you ever had a child with him.

BEING A GOOD PROVIDER DOESN'T MAKE HIM A GOOD FATHER

Just because he provides for his children by putting a roof over their heads, food on the table and puts clothes on their backs doesn't mean he's a good dad, it just means he's a good provider, even if he is a hard worker. Throwing money at his kids doesn't mean anything if he's not initiating quality time or investing in them emotionally. I know plenty of guys who throw money at their kids but can't even tell you when their children's birthdays are.

For the most part, men who throw money at their children but don't invest in them emotionally feel that they've done their job and have fulfilled their duties as a father. Now, don't get me wrong because with all the children in the world running around with no daddy's and all the deadbeat fathers who come up with ways to avoid paying child support it's a great thing to see a dad providing financially for his kids. However, the truth is that it still means very little if these children have no real emotional guidance or validation from their father.

DO YOU SPEND MORE TIME WITH HIS KIDS THAT AREN'T YOURS THAN HE DOES?

I know of so many situations where men who have kids that they've fathered with other women won't make effort to spend any time with them, but the woman they're currently in a relationship with always makes an effort to spend time with his kids that aren't hers.

So many women find themselves in this situation, especially if she has a child with that man. She'll want her child to know his or her other brothers and sisters and that's perfectly OK. She'll be the one taking them to the amusement/water parks and Chucky Cheese. She'll be the one who takes them to the movies and roller-skating. She'll be the one who buys them birthday and Christmas presents, and she'll be the one who tries to include them in on as many activities as possible. In the end she'll be closer to his kids and baby's momma than he is.

It's not that there's something wrong with you including your child's other brothers and sisters in family activities, but the bottom line is if he were a real man he would be doing these things, not you, he wouldn't be letting you do his job.

First, this makes him a bad father, and second, if he were really in love with you he wouldn't be exercising this type of behavior because he wouldn't want you to have a negative outlook on him. He would want you to think of and know him as a good father who loves his kids. He'll make an effort to be a better father in his children's lives. You see, when a man falls in love with a woman she automatically brings out all of his positive, loving feelings, and he'll change his attitude. Also, he'll want to pass those feelings on to the ones he loves, especially his children. If he's not trying to be in his other children's lives, it's because he doesn't care about his children or what you think.

DON'T BELIEVE HIM WHEN HE SAYS THE REASON HE DOESN'T SPEND TIME WITH HIS OTHER CHILD IS BECAUSE HIS BABY'S MOMMA MAKES IT HARD FOR HIM. THAT'S ALL BULLSHIT! HE DOESN'T SPEND TIME WITH HIS CHILD BECAUSE HE DOESN'T WANT TO!

Nothing, and I mean nothing can keep a man from being with his child if he wants to be. A real man does whatever he has to do to be with his child, and nothing, including an out of control drama queen baby's momma is going to keep him from his child.

I used to know a guy that would walk four miles in the snow three times a week so that he could spend time with his baby girl. I asked him how does he do it without freezing, and he responded, "Freezing is a small price to pay to spend time with my baby girl; I'd walk ten miles if I had to." That's the way it should be.

Men make up all kinds of excuses about why they don't spend time with their children, but the bottom line is a man doesn't spend time with his children because he doesn't want to and he doesn't care, that's the truth. The baby wasn't planned, he was just too lazy to get a condom or pull out, the next thing you know a baby is here. In his mind it took no effort to make this child, which makes him nothing more than disposable sperm, so the child means very little to him.

I know plenty of fathers who always find the time to go out to the clubs and take girls out to dinner and hang out with the fellas, but the thought of spending real quality time with their child is an inconvenience to them. What's so fun about hanging out with a child that he has no emotional connection with? Is this really the type of man you want to be with?

NOT ATTACHED TO THE MOM MEANS NOT ATTACHED TO THE CHILD

So many guys have sex with girls that they're not in love with or have any feelings for, whether it's a booty call, a one-night stand or just two friends or associates who decided to hook up.

In these situations where the girl gets pregnant, the man's first response is to detach himself from the girl and keep minimal contact with her as possible. After all, in his mind this is her problem, not his. *Why doesn't she get an abortion and leave me alone?* As long as he doesn't acknowledge the situation or respond to her he's not responsible, so he thinks? The last thing this guy ever wanted was to have a baby with this particular girl, but again, no condom, no pull out equals baby.

Unfortunately for the baby, because this guy has no connection with the mom, he has no interest in having a relationship or bonding with the child. *What's the difference, it's still his baby*? You might be thinking, but it doesn't matter because when a girl tells a guy that she's pregnant with his child he only has one thing on his mind, and that's how this pregnancy will affect him. He'll be damned if he's going to turn his life upside down because a woman he doesn't give a shit about said she's pregnant with his baby! So, the easiest thing for him to do is emotionally walk away. The only time he'll give much thought to the baby is when Uncle Sam is taking money out of his paycheck. That is unfortunate for the child.

YELLING AND CUSSING AT HIM WON'T MAKE HIM BE A BETTER FATHER

So many females yell and holler at their baby's daddy's about what they're not doing, whether it be spending time with the child, helping out with the bills or just helping out period. Save your vocal cords. If he cared he would always be on his job by initiating and doing his part and also calling you to see what else he can do for the baby and you. He's not doing anything because he doesn't care and doesn't want to, so screaming and chastising him won't make a difference or get a reaction out of him. Save your breath.

EVEN IF HE'S LIVING OUT OF STATE, HE CAN STILL CALL DAILY OR EVERY OTHER DAY

It doesn't matter if he's living out of state, a real man who wants to be a part of his child's life will at least call every day or every other day. He'll still be a dad, still discipline, praise and stay in constant communication with his child. If he cared, he'd want to know how his child is doing regularly, make sure the child is doing their homework and listening to their mother. He's also always making sincere plans to have his child fly out to stay with him for the summers and holidays. No real man can stand to be away from his child for too long. I tell you right now, if your baby's daddy isn't making these kinds of efforts with your child, then he doesn't care.

THE BOTTOM LINE:

The bottom line is these men don't care about the child or you. You're just an inconvenience in his life, and the easiest thing he can do is to distance himself as much as possible if not altogether from both you and the child. That doesn't mean he'll be mean about it, but that's how he feels. He has as much interest in being in this child's life as he does wanting to run a marathon. In the end, all it comes down to is whether that child is going to want a relationship with his/her father when they're older. When the child becomes older, either he'll/she'll care less about pursuing a relationship with their father, or will feel like something is missing from their life as they're entering their adult years and want to get to know their real father and build a relationship. In the end, they'll make the decision.

37

WHY MEN WON'T DATE WOMEN WITH KIDS

He never really liked you in the first place, that's all. No man has ever looked at a woman and thought to himself, *She stills my heart, her smile rocks the core of my soul, she's an angel from heaven, she's the epitome of beauty, but too bad she has kids or I would date her.* No, it doesn't work that way. Either we like and are attracted to you or we're not, period, regardless of your children. Ideas are floating around why a man won't date a woman with kids, and some of them are.

1. He doesn't want to deal with the financial responsibility if it gets serious.
2. He doesn't want to raise another man's child.
3. She has too much extra luggage.
4. All of her kids have different baby's daddies and that's a turnoff.
5. He doesn't want to deal with baby daddy drama, and the list goes on.

The only men who are going to say these things are the ones who never really liked you from the beginning, never had any real plans on courting you and never wanted to be in a relationship with you in the first place.

HE'LL MAKE THE SINCERE EFFORT

When a man meets you, and he likes you, all he wants to know is what is it going to take for him to spend more time with you. He's looking forward to basking in your presence for many more days to come. So when you tell him that you have a child or children, believe it or not he's happy about that. I'll repeat it, he's happy about that. Why? Because the first thing that'll pop into his head is, *All I have to do is show her how good I am with her kids and I'm officially in the door.* Trust me, we all think this way when we really like a woman and we find out that she has kids. Don't forget, we want to be with you, and the only way to be with you in our minds is by impressing you. What better way to impress you than by showing you how good we are with your kids. All of a sudden we'll become Mrs. Doubt Fire. We'll bring them gifts when we come over, take' em to the park or Chuckie Cheese, help them with their homework, make' em laugh, sit up and watch movies with them. Whatever it takes to impress you we'll do it. When we're gaga over you, we can't wait to show you how good we are with your kids.

Now, before you think that I'm talking about a man using your kids for personal gain, I'm not. The fact that he is doing all of these things with your kids means that he is a decent man who likes to see them have fun and enjoy themselves. He recognizes because he wants this to work with you that they'll be a part of his life as well. No matter how dumb we are all men know that the most important thing in a woman's life is her children. If we can't show you that we can be a good father figure for your kids, then that means you and him are not moving on to phase two. Phase one was getting you to like him, and phase two is earning your trust.

WHEN THE RELATIONSHIP IS OFFICIAL

So remember, if he's in love with you he'll also love the most important thing in your life, your children. A man can't be in love with you and not love your kids. If he makes no real effort to be in your children's lives, tries to bond or spends any real quality time with them, then he's not in love with you. Either being in a relationship with you is convenient for him for the moment or you're just something to do for right now, even if you're married.

Don't ever think that a man lost interest or wasn't interested in you because you have kids. He just wasn't serious about you in the first place.

38

HE ALWAYS PUTS MY FAMILY ON THE BACK BURNER

YES, IT'S TRUE; MOST GUYS DON'T WANT TO SPEND TIME WITH THEIR IN-LAWS

Let me say that most guys don't want to spend time with their in-laws or even people that they don't have anything in common with, that's a given. It has nothing to do with how great they are as people. Guys don't like to be in a position where they have to force conversation or converse topics they don't care about. Nine times out of ten we'd rather be somewhere else or doing something else. However, if he were really in love with you and because he knows that it would make you happy he would find and make the time to spend with your family. He knows that even though these are people and circumstances that he would rather not entertain or be around, because it's important to you, it'll become important to him. A man in love wants to make you happy, and if spending time with your family for a few hours makes you happy, then he'll grow a pair. No, he's still not going to participate in all the family events, but he'll make an effort to participate in as much as he can. He'll use that time with your family so he can get in their good graces and in return he would want them to remind you of what a great man you have and how lucky you are to have found him.

If he were really in love with you it wouldn't have even gotten to this point where you have to battle with him about this matter. The fact that it has gotten to this point means he's already offended your family and they got the message that he doesn't want to be around them. You can only make up so many excuses to your family about him working late or overtime. No man in love wants to offend the family of the woman he plans to marry. The simple fact that he makes no effort to redeem himself in the eyes of your family means flat out that he doesn't care about your family's perception of him, especially as a new member of the family. The reason he doesn't care about their perception of him is because he isn't in love with you. Walk away!

39

HE WAS RAISED IN A FAMILY THAT DIDN'T COMMUNICATE, SO HE DOESN'T KNOW HOW

I had a friend who once said this to me about her husband. She was upset because whenever she wanted to discuss the problems they were having in their marriage he was always non-responsive or didn't contribute much to the conversation. I told her it has nothing to do with his upbringing or the fact that he grew up in a family that didn't communicate with one another, that's bullshit!

I tried to explain to her he's not making an effort to communicate because he doesn't want to, doesn't care, not in love with her, doesn't want to be married to her anymore and he's ready to move on. If he were in love with her the majority of their issues wouldn't exist in the first place. Whatever problems or issues they were having that needed discussing he would jump at the chance to fix them.

You have to understand, when a man in love sees any upset in his marriage he quickly wants to make things right again, because if he doesn't, you might consider walking away and leaving him, no way in hell can he have that!

He knows that if there's a problem in his marriage then his woman is unhappy, if his woman is unhappy then it's going to show in her behavior in how she talks to and responds to him. He'll pick up on this and realize she's unhappy about the way things are going, and his insecurities and doubts about how she feels about him will manifest in his mind, and that he might be losing her or pushing her away on account of what he is or isn't doing. As a result, he'll quickly rush to communicate and to make everything right and whole again in their marriage.

Again, if a man is in love, it usually won't even have to get to that point, especially if you're properly communicating with him, he'll communicate with you. So don't let him use his upbringing as an excuse for his non-communication skills. After all, your man can sit there and communicate all day with other men about sports, hunting, fishing, cars, their jobs and playing video games, but when it comes to his marriage/relationship that's in jeopardy, all of a sudden he doesn't know how to communicate? Bullshit! Again, he's not making an effort to communicate because he doesn't want to, doesn't care, not in love, doesn't want to be in a marriage with you anymore and he's ready to move on, so should you. Walk away!

40

BUT HE INTRODUCED ME TO HIS FAMILY?

Women want to believe because a man introduces them to his family and close friends that there's meaning behind it, and he wants to settle down or be monogamous with them, sometimes yes, sometimes no. I've introduced a lot of women to my parents and family members, and it only meant something maybe once or twice.

When it comes to guys bringing a woman around our people whom we're not serious about, sometimes we can be complete sociopaths. We can bring a woman around our folks and they can like her and talk about how great and beautiful she is and we could care less. In our minds she just came along for the ride. She could be nervous as hell or even a bit uncomfortable because she doesn't know what to expect or consumed with trying to make a good impression, but, in our minds, it's just not that serious.

It doesn't mean we're trying to be an ass toward you, but by him bringing you around his family is the equivalent of bringing one of his good buddy's over to meet his folks, "Hey, what's up mom, dad, Aunt Lucy, this is Tina or Franky." It just doesn't click to a guy most of the time that it's usually a bigger deal to you than it is to him, and that you're going to read more into it, especially if he's stringing you along with no real intent on a future for the both of you.

41

BUT WE HAVE SO MUCH HISTORY TOGETHER

I hear women say this all the time, "But we have so much history together."

How much history, how much time, how long you've known each other, and the tender moments that you've shared only mean something to a woman, it means little to a man. Guys don't care about the length of time that you two have been in each other's lives because guys don't think that way.

Women live in a world of feelings and emotions, so women tend to hold on to shared, intimate, connected moments and just the past in general. For a man, it's not so much about the history that you two have shared, but the bottom line is, does he desire you right now? Guys live in a world of, "either it is or it ain't." In other words, no matter how it was or used to be between you two, a man is only thinking, *Would I put myself back in that situation again? Am I still attracted to her? Do I still want her? Do I still see a future with her? I'm tired of the arguing, she put me through too much the last time we were together.*

Regardless of what he thinks about your history, in the end, if he wanted to be with you he'd be fighting for you and your relationship.

DOES HE STILL THINK ABOUT ME?

Basically what you're hoping is for him to realize the bond and all the positive moments and beautiful memories you two have shared in the past. And you're hoping that'll be enough to make him want to come back and rekindle the relationship. You're also hoping if you play that love song enough times that eventually he'll telepathically feel your thoughts and emotions and come crawling back to you.

Yes, of course your ex thinks about you from time to time and about some of the great moments you two have shared, and yes sometimes he can even miss them. But that's just it, he'll miss them, meaning the good times, not necessarily you. Remember, missing the positive moments is different than missing you. A lot of times a man calls up his ex whom he hasn't spoken to in a while because he's a little depressed or feeling low. He's not calling her because he misses her directly, but wants reminding of a time when he used to laugh and feel good. And since you two have once shared that together, of course you're the right candidate for a picker-upper or booty call.

Sometimes when two people who have history together break up, haven't seen each other for a while and so much time has passed they can start to miss some of those great moments they've shared. But, once you sit down and have a conversation with that person, you're reminded why you broke up with them in the first place. You start to see some of those negative characteristics that turned you off or pushed you away coming back in their conversation. Some of those negative characteristics you can overlook and some of them you can't get past.

So when you say, "We have so much history together," it means nothing to a man. I'm telling you there's a reason why your relationship is history, there's a reason your thoughts are from the past, because that's where they should stay, the past! There are a lot of great guys out there who you can be making new memories with and who'll love you. Holding on to a dead past that doesn't want you anymore is holding you back from creating a future with your real Mr. Right!

42

THERE'S SOMETHING ABOUT YOU PHYSICALLY THAT TURNS HIM OFF

Unfortunately, we live in a superficial society where looks and physical appearances play a significant part in how a man does or doesn't respond to you. No, I'm not talking about breasts.

It usually consists of something irreversible. Either way this chapter may touch a nerve.

SOMETIMES A MAN CAN'T HELP BUT BE SUPERFICIAL

Many men have had great women in their lives. Women who were loving, smart, wife/relationship material, and they were attracted to these women, but, there was just one thing about them physically that turned them off that these men couldn't get past.

Now, because of that physical flaw she had, his attraction and feelings for her never went to the next level. Sometimes a man tries to get past it and focus on her other great qualities, but, eventually, that superficial devil sits on his shoulder and starts talking in his ear, *look how big her forehead is, why is her ass so flat? Her eyes are spread too far apart; she'd be perfect if her teeth weren't so long,* and so on. I know it may seem superficial and insensitive but it is a reality. Chris Rock said it best, and I quote, "When it comes to dating or being in a relationship, you just can't love the white part of the bread, but you also have to love the crust."

HE'LL NEVER TELL YOU BECAUSE HE DOESN'T WANT TO HURT YOUR FEELINGS

He'll never tell you he has a problem with your, "Physical flaw," because he doesn't want to hurt your feelings. Sometimes he'll drop little hints. For instance, if you put on a few pounds and you mention it and say something like, "Maybe I should start going to the gym," he'll say, "Oh baby, you're fine just the way you are! But, if you want?" but, in the back of his mind he's thinking, *I'll personally drive you there.* If he's dropping hints and you're not catching them eventually he'll either cut out dating you because he knows there's no chance of his feelings for you going to another level and he doesn't want to hurt you any more than you will be. Or, he'll continue to date and sleep with you while weighing his options, or until something better comes along.

IS YOUR PHYSICAL FLAW REVERSIBLE?

If what he sees as a physical flaw is reversible and you have other strong qualities, whether they be mental or physical, to him, they are more than likely physical, then sometimes in a guy's mind he'll decide that he'll quote-unquote "Work with you," if you're willing to work on the problem. For example, let's say you have too many stretch marks, but he likes everything else about you, well he knows that there are creams and medical laser technology that can reverse it. Or if your teeth are a little yellow or not as white as they could be, he knows they can be whitened, or if you're overweight, he knows with exercise you can lose it and be hot, or just presentable. I'm not trying to say that you look like some deformed monster because your "flaw" can be simple, but still, he won't get past it. If it's reversible, in his mind, he'll work with you.

DON'T CHANGE WHO YOU ARE

It's not a question of changing who you are, but being patient enough to wait for the right man who wants to fall in love and be with you.

Just because one guy can't get past what he sees as a physical flaw in you, there are two more that won't have a problem with it. Remember, when one man only sees a piece of coal when he looks at you another man only sees a diamond. Another man's garbage is another man's treasure. Of course I'm not calling you garbage, but what one man throws away and will be embarrassed of, another man takes that same piece and sets it on his mantle for everyone to see.

I had a friend who broke up with his woman because he said she had too many stretch marks, another man came along and swept her off her feet, and now they're happily married. He treats her like a princess, with stretch marks and all. See how that works?

IN CLOSING

Remember, it doesn't matter how nice, sweet or caring you are, sometimes a guy can't get past what he perceives as a physical flaw in you, and you need to move on. You won't know it's because of the physical flaw and unless he hints about it there's no real way of telling. If he's not treating you the way you should be treated according to the standards I'm setting in this book, then you need to walk away!

43

HE MAKES NO EFFORT TO SATISFY YOU IN BED

A man who's in love won't be selfish in the bedroom. What's true is some men can have an intimate relationship with a woman for a long time and still not even be aware that she's not completely satisfied or even having orgasms unless she's faking it. Sometimes it doesn't mean that a man's selfish; it just means that he doesn't know any better. Sometimes a woman has to put the brakes on and say, "STOP! This isn't working; let me show you how to do this the right way." After she teaches him a thing or two he'll work at becoming a better lover, again, if he's in love with her.

I USED TO BE YOUR HUSBAND

The truth is when it comes to sex, coming up, males just wanted to hunt and conquer. We didn't care about a female's body and her needs, how to caress her or how to kiss her softly. We didn't know precisely where the sensitive areas of her breast were, or even how to give a female a gentle massage. Taking the time to make sure she is satisfied orally? forget about it, most guys wouldn't even touch that area with their mouths. These weren't exactly things that guys talked about with each other or were shown to us. When I was coming up, I used to be big on just trying to get on top of a woman and get the job done as soon as possible so that I could move on. A female's pleasure was certainly the last thing on my mind. I'm not trying to sound crude, but I never thought it was important for a woman to be satisfied in bed. I thought as long as she knew that I was satisfied then she was satisfied because she did her job. I couldn't care less about making sure a woman was relaxed, comfortable or stimulated. I didn't even know where the clitoris was until I was in my twenties. But, the more I began maturing, evolving and growing up, I began to fall in love, and from there, I began to listen to the woman I loved. What does she want, what makes her feel good, where and how long should I touch her there?

The bottom line is if a man isn't taking the time to please his woman sexually and even learn her body then he's not in love with her.

THIS IS WHAT I MEAN

Let me explain to you about the mindset of a man in love who knows he isn't sexually satisfying his woman.

His insecurities will get to him. He'll begin to feel self-conscious because he can't please his woman the way he would like. All of a sudden he'll begin to concern himself less with his satisfaction and focus more on how he can please her. Not only will he begin to ask her questions about what she would like, but he'll also be more open to suggestions and comments from her. Some women think that criticizing their man about his sexual performance will break any confidence he has, but the truth is, when he's in love he wants you to speak up and say something because he doesn't know. Anything you can do to make his job easier he'll appreciate it.

You have to remember that part of a man's sexual arousal is knowing that his woman is being pleased, and he loves the sounds of her moans, screams and the way she moves her body during the love making. It gets a man even more excited when he's making his woman lose control. When a man's in love, he wants to take his woman's satisfaction to another level. No man in love ever wants to feel like he isn't doing his job in the bedroom because he knows there's somebody else out there that will, if his woman has a mind to cheat or leave him altogether.

The bottom line is if you've been telling your man that you're not satisfied, and you've been telling him what you would like and what he can do to stimulate and please you more, and he still makes no real effort to oblige, that's his simple way of saying, "I'm not in love with you, so your pleasure and satisfaction isn't important enough for me to make an effort."

HE'LL EXPERIMENT FOR YOU

It doesn't matter if your man isn't the adventurous type in bed. If you want to try new positions, bring in toys, role-play, even bring in a third party or whatever little experimental ideas you have, even if he's not with it all the way, a man in love still experiments and tries new things with his woman. It's what you want, and he knows it'll please you. He might not do everything you suggest, but he'll open himself up to more than half of your ideas. If he's not even trying to be open-minded to your ideas of new sexual adventures, then he's not in love with you.

No, I'm not saying that just because your man won't try something new that he's not in love with you. I'm saying that when a man's in love, his love for you makes him come out of his comfort zone.

44

DON'T WORRY; HIS ERECTILE DYSFUNCTION IS NOT A REFLECTION ON YOU

The truth is, a man can be sexually attracted to you, you can be butt naked in bed, looking/smelling good and dry humping each other to death and he still won't be able to, "Get it up." This is very common, and it happens all the time to many men.

What is true, is routine and redundancy in the bedroom gets old and isn't very motivating. However, no matter how routine it is it won't stop a man from getting an erection with you. Even if we're not in the mood we can still get it up because the bottom line is we still want to fire one-off. So what that means is something else is going on with him.

I understand how it can make a woman feel undesirable, unattractive and like her man is just sexually bored with her, but believe me it's not you; it's him.

IT'S IN HIS MIND

A man can have a lot of things going on in his mind that can cause him not to get an erection; it can be stress, worry, fear, anxiety, depression, etc. Also, when you think that he's not showing any of those symptoms it can be subconscious, something going on in the back of his mind like guilt or uncertainty. Nothing is a bigger cock blocker than the mind.

IT'S ALSO IN HIS BODY

There are so many things going on in his body that can cause him not to have a proper erection like having thyroid issues and even just getting older. I had a friend who was having an erection problem for years who was a big coffee drinker. When he finally went to the doctor to get some answers, it turned out that all the caffeine he was consuming was the problem. Once he cut out the caffeine he got his erection back. A man's diet can be a significant contributing factor.

I remember after having gallbladder surgery, they put me on a specific medication that not only killed my erections, but it was also hard for me to urinate. The point is, sometimes it can be what's going on in his body or what he's putting in his body.

I'm not a doctor or certified so my advice would be to go online and read up on erectile dysfunction and also have him see a doctor.

YOU STILL GOT IT!

Again, many things can cause erectile dysfunction that has absolutely nothing to do with you. So don't ever think that it's a sign that you're not attractive or you're losing your touch, it has nothing to do with that.

45

WHAT MEN REALLY THINK ABOUT YOUR BREASTS, BIG AND SMALL

You poor women. For years you have let TV and entertainment brainwash you into believing that big breasts are more serious and significant to guys than they really are. Trust me; big breasts are not as important to us as you think. I'm not trying to patronize you by saying, "Well, your breasts are kinda small, but that's OK because I still like you for who you are." No, that's not what I'm talking about at all. I'm saying that we are not into big breasts the way TV says we are. Yes, I understand that you women see images of women on TV/online with these big knockers and guys are just hooting and hollering over them. I understand that you have a co-worker with big boobs who seems to get more attention than you do. I also understand that your girlfriend who has a big pair of double D's always seems to get approached more than you do when you two are out in public. I get it.

The only reason you see your girlfriend and co-worker with big boobs getting more attention and approached more than you is because their breasts are highlighted and popping out more. Meaning they're more in your face and blunt than a woman whose breast are smaller. Because to men breasts are sexual objects and when they're more in your face they make us think about one thing, sex! So when we see a woman with big breasts in public we're not responding to her breasts, we're responding to what her breasts represent to us and what we like to think of, again sex! That's all. Trust me on this. If you were to come to work with your small breasts wearing nothing but a t-shirt and panties do you think for a second that the men at your job will be staring at the woman who's fully dressed with the big boobs, hell nah! Why? because again, big boobs make us think about sex, but now you just took it to another level and sent our sexual thoughts into overdrive.

As men, we're always thinking about sex in some form or another, and we're always looking and analyzing women's bodies where ever we are. That doesn't mean that we're longing or drooling over them, it's just our nature to discreetly give women's bodies an overview when we're out in public or when we first meet them. We stare at tits and ass all the time, especially when they're big. That's because big breasts and big asses are unique in the sense that you're not guaranteed to see them every day, so when we do see them, yes, they'll momentarily hold our attention. And when we're at the grocery store and an attractive woman is coming down the aisle with big boobs we're going to look at her unique features. Of course I don't mean stare at her like a weirdo, but a quick glance outta the corner of our eye.

BIG BREASTS DOESN'T EQUAL BETTER SEX

It's true, big breasts doesn't equal better sex for guys, just like a woman knows that just because a guy has a big penis it doesn't always mean that it's going to be pleasurable. Most guys, as they get older, tend to realize this about big breasts. The media taught guys that big breasts were something special and having sex with a woman with big breasts was like entering a new magical world with wonders and awe. As we get older we start to realize that it doesn't always enhance or make the sex better one way or the other. She could have beautiful big breasts and the sex could still be nothing special. That's because for the most part, like any form of sex and pleasure, after awhile big boobs tend to lose their novelty.

YOUR SMALL BREAST ARE JUST GREAT!

While watching a talk show on TV one afternoon, the women on stage were discussing women's breast sizes. During the Q and A one woman from the audience made a very insecure comment about herself. She said she feels that the men who date her secretly wish that her breasts were bigger and fear they'll eventually get tired of her small breast and pursue other options. She also said that the men she dates never indicated that they had any problem with her small chest, but she's so insecure about her size that she'll break it off with these men before they can dump her. That is so sad because she's not alone. Millions of women feel that way about their breasts. In many ways the media tells you that you're only as valuable as your bra size. I'm here to tell you that it's not true. When a man falls in love with you, it's with you, not your bra size. It's you as a person that we want, your love, nurturing, friendship and partnership is what seals the deal. Not the temporary illusion. Because again, as dumb as we are all men know that in the long run we need an emotional connection, not a physical connection.

YOUR BREAST LOOK GOOD ON YOUR BODY

For guys, a woman's breast has to look good on her body and her body alone. Some women's bodies look good with a B cup and some look good with a C cup, etc. In other words, every woman's body wouldn't look good with big boobs. Your breast looks good when proportioned to your body.

As men evolve, we learn for the most part that it's not the "Thing" itself that we're attracted to, but it's the "Person" who the "thing" is attached to that makes them special and unique.

I was dating a sista named Lynda years ago. This woman was sexy! And of course I could see she wasn't big breasted, maybe a small B cup. I was attracted to her and just found her body so damn sexy. Her smooth chocolate skin, her smile and her lovely hips and round butt was doing it for me, moving on. On the first night we were intimate, while fooling around, I went to pull her shirt up over her head and she stopped me. I just figured that she was giving me a red light that she wasn't ready to go too far. As the kissing and petting continued, I attempted to pull her shirt off again, and again she stopped me. I asked her if anything was wrong, and she responded by saying, "I'm embarrassed because my breasts are small." Of course she was right, her breasts were small, and so what? They were also sexy as hell, smooth, chocolate, and nice nipples. She was very insecure about her size. I had to explain to her that her breasts were perfect for her body shape and size. I also had to explain to her that what made her breasts sexy was because they were hers. I was so attracted to her and found her so damn sexy that everything about her was good to me, including her small breast. In other words, it's not the breast that makes you sexy, it's the woman they're attached to, big, small, whatever. Yes, her breasts were small, but they were the sexiest breasts that I had seen in a long time, also, because again, they were hers. What she didn't realize was that big breasts wouldn't look good on her frame and her small breast looked great on her body.

However, I've also been with women with spectacular big breasts. For example, I dated a woman named Sue, who had the most beautiful breasts that I had seen on any woman in my life. She was a caramel sista with double D breasts. When naked, her breasts were firm, stood up on their own, lovely nipples, areolas, and no scars. She just had phenomenal breasts. I used to tell her that she could easily be a breast model. But, it wasn't just because they were big that made them nice, they were just nice big breasts that looked good on her body and frame period.

Here's a head-scratcher, even though she had the most beautiful most spectacular breasts that I had ever seen, they were not sexy. I know you're thinking, "What does that even mean, spectacular but not sexy?" It means when it comes to your body parts, no matter how good they look, it doesn't always make them sexy. However, Lynda's small breasts were very sexy. Lynda was just sexier period, small breasts and all. Also, Sue's big breasts wouldn't have looked good on Lynda's body and vice versa. They each had beautiful breasts but their breasts looked good on their bodies. As men, we respond to each woman's breasts differently and it has nothing to do with their size.

COME ON NOW, I KNOW THAT MEN LIKE BIG BREASTS MORE THAN YOU'RE ADMITTING

Of course, some men love big breasts and are breast men. Just like they're men with foot fetishes, ass men, leg men, etc. Sexual attractions, desires and fetishes come in all shapes and sizes. There are a lot of men who like to feel the fullness and roundness of a woman's big breasts in their hands and do things to them with their mouths. The point is, that's for men who are fond of big breasts. However, that doesn't make up a large part of men in our society. I'm merely pointing out that the big breast standard in our society is exaggerated by TV and for the most part is false. It's not a necessity or as relevant when it comes to the real average guy and what he looks for in a woman. No matter what size they are, big or small, beautiful breasts are beautiful breasts and are only as appealing as the woman they're on. Trust me.

46

HOW NOT TO REPRESENT YOURSELF ON DATING AND SOCIAL SITES

"I like my woman classy, not showing all the assy!" That quote was from Martin Lawrence on an episode of Martin. As you're going to learn from reading this book I watch a lot of old sitcoms. But, that quote has everything to do with this chapter.

Take it from a former player who has slept with hundreds of women. I always appreciate a beautiful body on a woman. But, putting pictures of yourselves on social websites, flashing your asses in tight pants and exposing your cleavage with a smile on your profile page will get you nowhere fast. Also, showing your ass from the side or back so we can get a good look at your curves looks ridiculous, you know who you are.

Listen, no real man of quality or substance is going to respond to these pictures or you, but the ones who respond are the ones who are looking for a piece of ass. They're only thinking, *"I'd like to hit that shit!"* and when they're done hitting it 3 or 4 times they're going to move on. Your suggestive pictures and poses will only lead to disappointment.

A man knows that a **real woman** with **confidence** and a **high opinion** of herself is not going to start her initial presentation with her ass and breasts all up in the camera. A real woman with confidence doesn't need to try and dangle the carrot to make the horse come to her. Instead, she presents herself as a lady and carries herself as such, and that's the quality that makes men want to wine and dine you. It's always more attractive and sexier when a woman with a nice body and smile is more reserved and carries herself with some sense of class, not a woman who's showing her body and acting like an 18-year-old wannabe stripper. I'm not hatin on you, a lot of you women with these photos look good and are women men wouldn't mind tappin, but outside of tappin it no man is going to take you seriously. Less is more, and men would rather see you cover your sexy breasts and make us wonder what's underneath there. When we see you flashing your ass at the camera or giving us the side view, it just makes us think of one thing, "*Immature.*"

YOU ARE WEAK!

As men, we see that type of behavior as a sign of weakness, like when the lions see the weak wildebeest on its last leg, what do they do? they attack and go after it to devour it. And when they're done having their way with it they leave the corps to rot. That's how men see you women with these sexual photos; you're fun to look at, but weak, and after they attack and devour you they're going to drop you. Long short is, present yourself as a lady and you'll get lady results, act like an insecure female who has to overcompensate by flashing and showing her breast and ass all up in the camera and you'll get insecure female results.

I'm not saying that just because you put a nice picture of yourself on your profile page that you're not going to attract idiots. I'm saying that if you present yourself by exposing too much on your site that you'll for sure only attract idiots. Then a few months later you'll be crying to your girlfriend and talking about why there are no good men out there.

Remember, as men, we make snap decisions and conclusions when it comes to the photos you put on your profile page, and smutty pictures tell a man everything he needs to know about you. But, if all you're looking for is a new booty call or some man to lay pipe, then yes, your ass and breasts pictures will work for that purpose.

Something else that's funny is some women like to put smutty pictures of themselves on social websites, but on their bios and interests they turn around and try to portray themselves as deep, insightful souls. They say things like, "I love poetry and romance. I love to read novels and take long walks in the woods." They say all of this as if this is supposed to balance out the smuttiness. It's ridiculous and comical. So get those breasts and ass pictures off of your page and present yourselves as the queens you are so you can meet your king. If not, you'll meet a lot of jokers and then you'll have no one else to blame but yourself.

47

ACT AND DRESS LIKE THE OLDER MATURE WOMAN THAT YOU ARE, IT'S SEXIER!

Years ago I worked for a retail store. The owner and my boss, Lynda, at the time was forty-three. She was a successful business owner with lots of money to throw around. Physically she was an attractive woman, sexy body and a pretty face. Lynda loved younger guys with hard bodies, boy toys. She was always doing everything to try and look younger because she felt she had to compete with the younger women that were also attracted to her boy toys. She always wore tight jeans, shirts that showed off her implants and belly button rings, too much makeup and tanned like it was a religion. I mean she would come to work looking like she dipped her face in tomato soup. She went to all the clubs and hot spots, partied hard and got shit-faced every weekend. Coke and X would keep her company from time to time. Point is she worked overtime trying to appear younger and hipper because she thought it would make her look more attractive to the types of younger guys she wanted. She was a classic case of insecurity and overcompensation. I just sat back and watched the train wreck but didn't say anything, because after all, she signed my paycheck.

One day while at work, she came up to me and started telling me her man problems. She told me how the guys that she dates always end up just using and dumping her and how no guy takes her seriously. Finally I had to say something to her. Even though my job could have been on the line, when it comes to giving women advice about men I don't hold back and I ripped into her. I responded sternly by saying, "It's because you're ridiculous!" She looked at me, shocked? I continued, "No real man is going to find you attractive and no real man is going to take you seriously when you're out there trying to fit in by partying, drinking and doing drugs every weekend. Lynda, you're a beautiful older woman, but you act like a teenager. With the way you dress and act, these guys can smell your need for approval coming a mile away. You have the right equipment, body/face, but your personality and presentation reeks of insecurity, neediness and no confidence. You would be so much sexier, desirable and attractive if you acted like a strong woman and carried yourself more like a lady. These younger guys would be lining up to throw their phone numbers at you if you acted like the successful, attractive business woman that you are. Get rid of those tight shirts that show off your breast implants, get rid of the tight-fitting jeans, stop tanning every other day and start dressing and looking like a real mature woman, then start acting like a real mature woman. Not only is it mentally healthier and better, but it's sexier. You want a real man in your life that's going to be good to you, younger or older, then it's time to make some changes!"

She didn't take too kindly to my comments. She also didn't fire me. But, from that day on, there was always a little strain in our work relationship. I quit after a year.

I ran into her a few years later at a convenience store. I was taken aback by her appearance. She was dressed in a cute outfit that looked right for her age. She was, do I dare say it, stunning! Also, when she spoke to me it was with a confidence that I had never heard from her the whole time we worked together. During the conversation she said to me, "You were right."

"Right about what?" I asked.

"About the advice you gave me three years ago. At first my feelings were hurt and I was offended, but when it started to sink in, I decided to make a change. Now I see the difference. Sometimes I still get approached by assholes, but I also get approached by a lot more men who treat me great." We talked a little more and shared a hug and said goodbye. I found her new ladylike appearance to be so attractive that for the first time since I've known her I almost asked her out. Lynda's gonna be OK.

ANGIE

Angie was the beautiful sexy wife on the George Lopez show. Her young hot niece, Veronica, was also beautiful and sexy and was staying with the Lopez family while going to college. On a Halloween episode Angie was feeling insecure about getting older and thought that her younger niece Veronica was way sexier than she was. Especially when she saw how George's friends made a big fuss over Veronica at the bar. The men whistled and hollered when Veronica walked in the room. This made Angie feel jealous and insecure; she also felt because she was getting older that she couldn't get that kind of a response from men anymore. So on the night that they were going to a Halloween party, Angie decided to overcompensate by dressing like a sexy nurse. George's friend came over to the house and when he saw Angie in her sexy nurse's outfit he got so turned on that he tried to downplay it by saying to her, "You look all right," like he wasn't impressed. Angie was so disappointed by his response that she took matters even further by cutting her short skirt even shorter, thinking this time she'll get a better response. Now she was really overcompensating. George told her she couldn't leave the house looking like that, but she was persistent about going to the party with her sexy outfit with or without his permission. She wanted to prove a point, and that point was she was still sexy and still had it! And she was going to that Halloween party so everyone else knew it. Long short, she and George talked it out and she never made it to the party.

The point is, what Angie didn't understand was, she didn't have to try and prove a point and dress up as a sexy nurse or be jealous of her younger niece Veronica, because she was already a hundred times hotter than her niece. Sure her niece was a sexy college girl, who could twirl any guy on her finger, but both women were sexy, hot, desirable and turned heads, but, Angie had one thing over her niece, and that thing was, she was an older woman. And a hot sexy older woman beats a hot sexy younger woman any day of the week, fact!

If George's friends could have had a choice of who they could have one night of passion with, they would have chosen Angie over her niece in a second, why? Because of what Angie represents to them, the older woman. You see when we were young, all guys had crushes on the older women in our lives, like our attractive baby sitter, our attractive school teacher, our friend's hot mom and

115

the hot mail lady that used to deliver in our neighborhood. You see, Angie's the fantasy, her niece Veronica wasn't. Sure they won't whistle or make a fuss in front of Angie's face, but behind her back they're making all kinds of gestures and talking about what they would love to do to her. Because even though guys are dumb, we still know that you can't treat a mature woman the same way you do a college girl. You can hoot and holler at a college girl but a mature woman you have to show some level of class if you expect to ever have a chance with one. Angie didn't understand that. She thought because the men weren't obvious about how attractive she was to them like they did her niece that it meant that she wasn't attractive at all. When in fact it meant the opposite, she was so attractive to them that they had to bite their lips until they bled. One, because she was a mature woman, and two, because she was George's wife.

So again, if you're a mature older woman, then carry yourself as such, with class and your sense of confidence. Because in the end it's much sexier!

48

WHAT MEN MEAN WHEN THEY SAY THEY WANT A CONFIDENT, INDEPENDENT WOMAN

When a man thinks of a woman with confidence that doesn't mean he believes she always has it all together or that she always knows what she's doing. Also, a confident woman doesn't always mean that she's strong or even independent. Being a confident woman has nothing to do with how much money she has or what she possesses materially. A confident woman to a man means that you know what yourself worth is, that's it! Having your own sense of identity and being self-actualized. You're not perfect, but you're comfortable with not being perfect. You're not moved by what everyone else thinks or by what everyone else is doing. You're focused on your own goals and dreams, and you have your own destiny and path to concern yourself with and not worried about what James or Kim is doing.

Before you think it's about money or material things that make the woman confident I'll let you in on a secret. Most of the women I've met with these positive qualities were women who didn't have a lot of money or material things. They were just regular women living day to day taking care of themselves and their children.

I've found that the women who have a lot of money and material things are some of the most insecure, timid, counseling needing, overcompensating women I have ever met. Of course not all women with money are like that, but the point I'm making is, to a man, a confident woman is about the substance she has on the inside, not the here today gone tomorrow stuff on the outside. The types of men who are initially drawn to women who are "Materially independent" and "doing her own thang!" soon realize that any woman can have money, but they usually want and need to be with a woman where there's an emotional connection. A perfect example of what I'm saying would be the 1996 Martin Lawrence movie "A Thin Line Between Love and Hate." Martin's character initially went after the woman with the money and the "Materially independent," lifestyle. But, in the end, his heart told him that he was in love with the woman who he shared an emotional connection with. Also, the woman whom he was in love with didn't have a lot of material possessions, but she was more confident and mentally stable than the woman who "had it all." So he followed his heart and went after the woman who didn't have the extravagant material lifestyle. If you haven't seen it, check it out, you'll get the point.

49

WHY DO MEN CHEAT?

I bet most of you, before even starting on page one skipped to this chapter to see what my response was going to be.

Well, I'm going to answer this question for you today, and no matter what any other man, therapist or your man himself tries to tell you don't believe or listen to any of them unless they're giving you the same answer that I am. But I know they won't.

Now the answer is not simple but very complicated. It has taken hundreds of years, thousands of hours of research to understand and to figure out the psychology of the male mind, the science behind the male human behavior and psyche. However, lucky for you today you get the answer to the most controversial question in the history of the male/female relationship. I know most of you females have been waiting patiently for this answer since you were young teenagers. Well, the wait is over! After all these years here's your answer as to why your man cheats. You ready? Here it is! Your man cheats on you, BECAUSE HE'S NOT IN LOVE WITH YOU!

That's it. There's your answer. Nothing more, nothing less. No big mystery. There's nothing else for you to understand or to figure out.

Your man cheats on you because he's not in love with you. I know you females were waiting for something more in-depth or some insightful, psychological mumbo jumbo reason as to why your man cheats, like he has trust or commitment issues, but that's all a bunch of bullshit. The simple fact is we cheat on women when we're not in love with them, that's it. In your case, HE'S NOT IN LOVE WITH YOU! Make peace with it and move on!

CHEATING WAS SO FUN THAT IT WAS BORING

Back in the day, I cheated on all of my past girlfriends and relationships. I don't mean just a few times, I mean it was all the time. Sex to me was just a sport, and the more girls I conquered in bed and sometimes in the car, the more I convinced myself into believing that this made me cool.

Now mind you, I was always good to all of my girlfriends, in the sense that I never abused them physically or verbally. I was funny and could make them laugh. However, I did abuse them emotionally. I never considered their feelings. I told so many lies to the point where it became a function.

I used to love to make them cry by acting like they said or did something wrong to me and pretending like I was going to leave or break up with them just to hear them beg me for another chance. You have to understand I was a real pretty boy in my prime and the girls loved me. It wasn't a big deal for me to tell one of my girlfriends to meet me somewhere and never show up or call. I was so conceited that I thought a female's only purpose in life was to wait for me to approach her, and for her to give me her phone number. It was just a cattle call situation to me.

There were times where I had so many different girlfriends that I would get tired and bored of trying to keep up with all of them, so I would play little games. Sometimes I would out myself and tell some of my girlfriends that I was cheating on them to see if I had enough game to make them want to stay with me, and in most cases they would. I would also leave little bread crumbs, like leaving phone numbers lying around, or I would have two girls meet me at the same place at the same time to see what the outcome would be. Yes, I got a sick thrill by fuckin' with their heads and playing mind games with them. Again, it was a sport.

CHEATERS DON'T DISCRIMINATE

I would even cheat on my girlfriends with their friends, and in some cases their sisters or cousins. There were times when I would have sex with one girlfriend at 7 p.m. then have sex with another girlfriend at 10 p.m. I have slept with over 200 females. Some who were even married? I used to have a list with all of their names and specialties and a ratings system. I'm not bragging, because that's nothing to brag about. Sometimes I look back and say to myself, "Over 200 females? What the hell was I thinking?" What's bad is out of over 200 women, I can probably remember no more than 15 or 20 of their names. Sometimes I rack my brain trying to remember a girl's name that I had sex with but come up empty. I see a face but no name. In other cases I see certain girls on the street or at the grocery store but I can't remember whether or not I had sex with them. Sure, they look familiar, and I think we had sex, but I'm not entirely sure. Things that make you go hmm?

It's sad to say but 200 girls isn't even a lot these days, because some guys I know are up in their 500 range easily, sad, but true. Let me stop rambling and start making some points here.

BOTTOM LINE IS, I WASN'T IN LOVE
WITH ANY OF THESE GIRLS

Now, you might listen to my stories of my past female exploits and think that I was an asshole; dog, scum, road kill and dirt, someone who deserved to have his dick cut off and thrown out of the car window. Regardless of what you think I did or how much I used, manipulated these girls and hurt them emotionally, it doesn't matter, because the bottom line is I wasn't in love with them.

Do you understand what I'm saying? It doesn't matter why I did these things and why I cheated on these girls, what mattered was that I was doing it, period. It doesn't matter why I'm not in love with you, I'm just not. Because of that it's no big deal for me to sleep with other girls while I'm supposed to be with you, Ms."You're just something to do for right now." You want to spend the next year and a half trying to figure me out? that's your problem. While you're wasting your brain cells thinking about me I'm in the house watching reruns of CSI and not thinking twice about you, unless I need something from you.

You see, I could pat myself on the back, brag about how much of a player I was, how much game I had, but it wouldn't be true. Because, the truth is, my game wasn't that strong, so why was I able to do all of these horrible things to these girls and mistreat them the way I had been? Because I was only doing what they were allowing me to do to them, you get it! Guess what? I never had a gun pointed at any of their heads, they could have walked away from me at any time and found a great guy who would have treated them right, but they chose on their own accord to stay with me, entertain and reap the consequences of someone who wasn't in love with them, and never would be.

No matter how many red flags I gave them, they wanted to hold onto me. They wanted to make it work with me. They wanted to hang in there with me. They wanted to believe that if they continued to put up with my unappreciative fucked up attitude that eventually I would learn to love and appreciate them in time. In the end, they got exactly what was coming to them, **nothing!** Because nothing is what you get when you invest your heart, time and emotions into a man who isn't investing his heart, time and emotions back into you. Ladies, do you truly understand me when I say walk away?

I WASN'T MATURE AND I HADN'T EVOLVED EMOTIONALLY AS A MAN

While I was out there running around and cheating on my girlfriends, the problem with me was, I wasn't mature and hadn't evolved emotionally as a man. I had a lot of great women at my disposal. Women who I could have been in loving, healthy, fulfilling relationships with. Instead of recognizing what I had in front of me I was only concerned with how I could use and manipulate these great and wonderful females for my self-centered purposes and needs.

You see, it doesn't always have something to do with the female herself, but sometimes a man hasn't matured enough emotionally to realize what he has. No matter how many women he beds, in the end all he gets is a cheap orgasm and an empty feeling. As he starts to mature emotionally, he'll begin to realize that he needs something more emotionally fulfilling because what he's been doing (sleeping around) isn't working anymore, or wasn't working to begin with. Sleeping with strange girls begins to feel cheap and unfulfilling to the point where he can hear that inner man telling him that something is wrong. After the sex is over he can't figure out why he slept with her in the first place. He feels disgusted. Not because there's something wrong with her, but because he realizes that he has no emotional attachment to this female, and without it, no matter how hot or fine she is, it's nothing more than a cheap physical act.

Guess what? I was that guy! I came to a place in my life of emotional maturity to where I realized I didn't want someone to fuck, I wanted someone who I could talk to, someone I could share my day and laugh with, someone I could eat Chinese food on the floor with while watching a movie drama. Most importantly, someone to love and take care of and in return, love and take care of me. I wanted more from a woman, not just sex; I've had plenty of that, but now I need something that I never had before, love.

Until a man reaches this point of emotional maturity and evolving in this area of his life, he has absolutely nothing to offer a woman, except disappointment and heartache.

MEN DON'T THINK WITH THEIR DICKS, THEY THINK WITH THEIR EGOS

A big misconception about men is, we cheat because we always need sex or have to be fuckin' all the time. Not true. Another big misconception is, we think with our dicks, again, not true. Ladies, men don't think with their dicks, they think with their egos. Again, for the un-evolved, emotionally immature male who isn't in love, sex is just about sport and conquering. That's the major of it. In football who gets the most attention, the player who makes the most touchdowns or the water boy who brings the fresh H20 and Gatorade to the players? Unless you're Adam Sandler in a mediocre football comedy the player scoring the touchdowns gets the most praise and attention. To use an early 90's saying, "He's the man!" Remember, men don't think with their dicks, but with their egos. Our egos tell us we have to try to sleep with this girl and that one and get as much pussy as possible. It's not just about the physical act itself, but the satisfaction we get from having our ego boosted by bedding another woman.

HE SAID HE CHEATED, BUT IT JUST HAPPENED

No, it doesn't just happen, duh. It's not as if he was blindfolded and was playing pin the dick on the home wrecker.

As men, we're so full of shit when we get caught cheating because sometimes we'll try to act like we're the victims in this case and we need someone to lick our wounds. "Baby, I'm so sorry for cheating, it just happened. She knows I'm this great and wonderful guy who's totally in love with his woman and she still took advantage of my caring, nurturing nature and seduced me into having sex with her. It just happened! I tried to walk away, but she used her succubus powers to pin me to the ground and continued to ride me up and down until she climaxed. Boohoo woe is fuckin me!" No, he screwed that girl because he wanted to. Before his dick ever came out of his pants he was in complete control. It doesn't just happen.

HE PROMISED IT WOULD NEVER HAPPEN AGAIN

If he were truly in love with you it wouldn't have happened in the first place, get it! Remember the movie Boomerang with Halle Berry and Eddie Murphy? Remember what she said before slapping the shit outta him, I quote, "Love should have brought your ass home last night!" When it comes to a man who's genuinely in love with his woman that statement is so true.

That doesn't mean he's above temptation or being curious, but he'll quickly come to his senses and love will bring his ass home. If love doesn't bring his ass home then he's not in love with you, period!

HE HAS WOMEN ON THE SIDE, BUT AT THE END OF THE DAY HE COMES HOME TO ME

If you're the kind of woman who knows her man is out there cheating and you validate it to yourself by thinking it's OK because at the end of the day he comes home to you, then you deserve what you get. Don't walk away, stay with him, because obviously that's all you're worth as a woman, just someone to come home to at the end of the day, after he spent the better part of his day with someone else.

HE'LL NEVER FIND ANYBODY AS GOOD AS ME

Some of you women believe this. Think about that for a moment. You're trying to express your value by telling him that he'll never find anybody as good as you. But, if you're allowing him to cheat and shit all over you, from his perspective, why is he supposed to look at you as a woman of value? You're right, he'll never find anybody as good as you, because he can find somebody better! A woman with a backbone who won't let him walk all over her and put up with his shit. Of course he'll fuck that relationship up too, but do you get the picture?

It's just as dumb when a woman asks, "Why can't men appreciate a good woman?" Simple! Date a good man and he'll appreciate a good woman. Keep dating idiots and you'll continue to be treated as such.

STOP BLAMING HIM! YOU'RE THE ONE WHO'S CHEATING ON YOURSELF

Let's cut the bullshit! Stop cheating on yourself and acting like this is the only man in the world. There are seven billion people in the world, and out of seven billion how many of them do you think are men?

Stop selling yourself short and acting like this is all you're worth or this is the best you can do. He ain't unique or special, you've just made him out to be in your head. He's a fuckin' man, and they're a dime a dozen. If he were in love with you he wouldn't have cheated or be cheating on you in the first place. Walk away!

50

HE'S BEEN HAVING SEXUAL ONLINE
CHATS WITH HIS EX BEHIND MY BACK

Your man isn't in love with you. If he were he wouldn't be having sexual conversations or allowing himself to receive sexual content from another woman as well.

After the very first sexual message he received from any woman he would have wrote back and said, "Look, I'm in a great relationship with so and so now, and if you can't respect that then we can't talk even as friends anymore. So stop sending me these sexual messages!" Your man probably won't say it that proper, but he'll get the point across.

If she continued to send explicit messages/texts to him, he would cut off communication with her period! You see, if your man were really in love with you he would be so scared of you ever finding out about these sexual messages he's been receiving that he would handle it right there on the spot and put an end to it. The reason is, because he wouldn't want you to get the wrong idea like he's been seeing another woman behind your back or put himself in a position that could jeopardize your relationship or make you lose trust in him. He would stop this immediately!

The reason this, "Sexual messaging" relationship continues between them is because you're not his real love interest or desire. Sadly, you're just someone he's set up shop with to be blunt. Yes, he's playing house with you, splitting the bills with you, going to your parents' house for Sunday dinners, laughing, having fun sex with you and might've even got engaged to you.

However, even if that's not the case and you're just simply his girlfriend, the mere fact that he's entertaining another woman in this way, even if it's just for a few minutes a day, means you don't have his heart and at this point you probably never will. He knows what he's doing is wrong and fucked up, but he's doing what he wants.

Walk away!

51

A MAN IN LOVE CAN EASILY HANDLE A LONG DISTANCE RELATIONSHIP

If you're in a long distant relationship and your man is living in another state or country for whatever reason, whether it be going to college, military, family or maybe his job requires him to leave for a year, whatever the case may be, if he cheats on you then he's not in love with you.

When a man is in love, being apart for an extended period or having to live in different states for the time being won't make him cheat. Your physical absence in his life causes his affections and love for you to grow stronger. Remember that old cliché saying, "Absence makes the heart grow fonder," well when you're in love, it does.

It also means that he'll be staring at your picture in longing every day. He'll want to call and text you as much as he can because you're always on his mind. Even though he's doing what he's supposed to be doing in his temporary new state or location, whether it be his job, school, military or whatever, his real motivation is to get back to you, his woman, his inspiration, his heart.

IF HE CHEATED ON YOU, IT'S NOT BECAUSE YOU'RE IN ANOTHER STATE

Seriously, it's not as if he was so in love with you, then all of a sudden he gets on an airplane and flies or drives seven hundred miles and temporarily has to settle in a new state for a while, then decides, "Wow, I don't think I'm in love with my woman anymore, well, time to get some new pussy." No, before he ever left his state he already knew that he wasn't in love with you and he was already planning or open to the idea of meeting new women before he reached his destination. That's why he's been sleeping around on your long-distance relationship and probably while he was in the same state as you.

HE CHEATED BECAUSE HE WAS LONELY AND MISSED YOU. BULLSHIT!

Don't ever believe a man when he says that while out of state he cheated on you because he was sad and lonely or because he missed you and he needed someone to be there for him and that other girl was there to fill the void. Yes, he did want female companionship, but not because he was sad, lonely, and missing you, but because he saw it as a chance to have another conquest in another state or location. That's the reason why he screwed the other girl.

YOU TWO HAVE BEEN ARGUING A LOT LATELY AND NOT GETTING ALONG. BULLSHIT!

Men love to use the, "We've been arguing a lot lately," excuse, especially when it comes to long-distance cheating. Here's the truth. When a man in love, who's out of state, hasn't talked to his woman for a few days or maybe even a few weeks because they've had an argument, no matter how mad he is and as long as your temporary separation isn't because you've cheated on him, within two to three days he'll begin to miss you, that's the truth.

At first he'll be mad, and then after a couple of days he'll start to miss you, but also try to convince himself that he doesn't. Then his mind will start to race because since you haven't made any contact with him his imagination begins to run away, he'll think that maybe he doesn't have the hold on you that he once had and maybe you're moving on. It'll begin to affect his sleep and his daily focus will be off, then the insecurities begin. Remember, when your man leaves you to travel there's always a little bit of insecurities that bounce around in his head. No matter how close or how much of a trusting relationship you two have a man still wonders if you're capable of cheating on him.

He'll begin to imagine you talking to another guy and the two of you have already been going on dates and spending time together. He'll think, maybe, just maybe, since you haven't called him or he hasn't called you, to get back at him you had a grudge fuck with the new guy and hell no he can't have that! Nobody is taking his true love away from him. Now he can't take it anymore. If he has to get on a plane or hitchhike back to the state you're in he will. From that point he'll pick up the phone and call. At first he'll try to act standoffish, but the truth is he doesn't want to argue and make it worse so he'll begin to turn into butter and let you know he misses you. Trust me; he's dying to make it right between the two of you again. This is how a man in love responds if he's had an argument with his woman who's in another state.

However, if you two have had an argument or a temporary fallen out while he was in another state, and in the process he cheats on you, walk away!

NOTE:

The same rules and principles apply even if you're the one who leaves to another state.

52

DOES HE ALWAYS KEEP HIS PHONE CLOSE TO HIM OR LOCKED?

This is a no brainer. He's cheating. Unless he's working for the FBI, no man in a real, loving, committed relationship has any reason to lock his phone or be secretive with it, especially around his woman. Whose number is in his phone that is so important that he has to keep it on lock status? It's not as if his messages contain secret government passwords or codes.

What's happening here is, he's hiding other girls or just one girl's text/voice messages and numbers from you.

SIGNS THAT IT'S ANOTHER WOMAN

1. When his phone rings or he receives a text in front of you, and he doesn't even respond or answers it.
2. When he doesn't text in front of you.
3. When he does text in front of you he'll text a lot faster.
4. When he answers the phone he won't talk in full sentences.
5. When he does check his text messages he does it fast. By the way, if he's secretly checking for her messages in front of you that means he really likes her.
6. A smart cheater gives her a ring tone that's a non-romantic/love song. It'll be something harder and edgier so he can say it's one of his boys or cousins calling. Or he puts her under a guy's name.

7. Of course, the standard giveaway, if he leaves the room after he receives the call or text. If he thinks he's clever, he'll wait a few minutes before leaving.

These are just some to name a few, and most are just common sense, but some women are in such denial that they won't be satisfied or convinced unless the other woman knocks on their front door holding a sign that reads, "I'm the one calling and screwing your man!"

WANT TO TEST YOUR MAN AND FIND OUT IF HE'S CHEATING ON YOU

Let's cut to the chase. Here's an easy test to find out if your man is cheating on you. The next time you two are in the house together, with a big smile on your face, spontaneously ask him for his phone, but don't tell him why you want it, and then ask him to leave the room for five minutes. If he can't do this simple, easy task, he's cheating on you.

Now, if he is cheating on you, not only will he not give you his phone, but he'll keep asking you why, "Why do you want my phone?" Then pretend to get mad or annoyed, start an argument or storm out, or pretend to give you the cold shoulder. No matter what he says or how much he bitches about you respecting his privacy or if he bitches about how come you don't trust him, either way, if he doesn't hand you his phone, he's cheating, that phone won't leave his pocket.

If he's not cheating on you he'll still ask you "Why do you want it?" and even think your request is odd, but he'll still play along, hand over his phone and leave the room. Even though he's not too sure as to what you're up to, he'll still have nothing to hide. Trust me, this test works, and I hope for your relationship he hands over his phone quickly.

A smart cheater deletes all of his messages as soon as he gets them from other girls. Lucky for the women in this day and age men are a lot lazier and leave all kinds of evidence and bread crumbs to get caught.

ARE YOU BEING AN OBSESSIVE CONTROL FREAK?

Now don't get me wrong, if your man is in love with you he can easily get turned off if you're the kind of woman who's so insecure that you always have to be checking his phone. He may not fall out of love with you but you run the risk of him having to check you on this matter or give you an ultimatum. That's why you can't do this test too often.

Sometimes you have to show some mental balance and restraint and not act like your man is cheating or isn't in love with you just because he doesn't say "Gesundheit," every time you sneeze.

Seriously, some of you need to get a grip, because if he were giving you that much insecurity then you don't need to be with him in the first place, right? If you have to check his phone like you have OCD then maybe you're the one with the problem. Truth be told if he's in love with you he's not going to give you a reason to have to look in his phone.

As for me, I'm the type of guy who doesn't lock my phone. I even leave it out while I'm sleeping. I'll gladly hand my phone over to my woman and let her roam all she wants. I'll even ask her to look up numbers on my phone for me if my hands are tied or if I'm driving. Now, that doesn't make me a saint, it just means I have nothing to hide. And by the way, if I did have to lock my phone for business reasons, you better believe my woman would be the only other person to have the password.

53

IF YOU WERE HANDLING BUSINESS IN THE BEDROOM HE WOULDN'T HAVE CHEATED?

The above statement is so untrue. Unfortunately so many women believe this. If a man is not getting sex when he wants it, or a certain kind of sexual favors from his woman, like if he wants to experiment or try something new or different in the bedroom, that won't make a man in love go out and cheat on her.

A man's love for his woman is not based on how well or how much she can throw down in the bedroom, or how much she's willing to push the sexual boundaries in your guys' relationship.

OF COURSE EVERY GUY HAS FANTASIES HE WANTS TO TRY

Every guy has fantasies and new sexual ideas that they would like to try with their woman, and some have fantasies that they are scared to talk to their woman about, out of fear that she might get turned off and push him away. Regardless, every guy, whether he likes it or not, understands that a woman isn't always into experimentation and trying new things or constant sexual activity. If she is willing to put out more or try new sexual activities she might not put her all into it and show a degree of hesitance.

At the same time, we as men feel that as long as our request isn't too out there or too kinky we expect our woman to be open-minded enough to at least consider the possibility of our request. Again, we also understand that sexual experimentation is different for every woman. For some women performing oral sex is a good thing and for others it's a complete nightmare.

Remember, he knew how you were before he fell in love with you, so it's not as if this is a surprise. Again, he's not going to cheat on you because you don't always want to experiment or you're not in the mood as much as he is.

BUT NOT SO FAST! THIS IS WHY A MAN IN THIS SITUATION STRAYS

If your man is in love with you and you're flat out withholding sex from him or always turning down his request to bring new ideas and games into the bedroom, what ends up happening is he'll eventually distance himself emotionally from you. Your man feels that if you were really in love with him, then you would be a lot more open to want to experiment, try new ideas with him and make love with him more than once a week, if that. After all, he's your man.

The fact that you're closed-minded and not making love to him as often as he would like makes him feel undesirable and unloved by you. Whatever reason you give as to why you don't want to, all he'll hear is, "I don't find you sexually attractive." As a result, he'll begin to look in other places to have his ego and sexual desires validated. Do you get that? It's not about what you're not giving him physically, but what you're not giving him emotionally. If you're not sexual with him, it makes him feel unwanted by you, unloved. It's not just a question of what you're not doing in the bedroom that'll make a man stray but your lack of communication. To use an old cliché, "Communication is the key."

54

MARRIED MEN, OR MEN IN RELATIONSHIPS WHO GO TO STRIP CLUBS

A man who is in love with you or any woman for that matter does not frequent strip clubs. Not only would we not disrespect our woman or our relationship in that way, but the desire to go to strip clubs isn't there. I know that they're women who say that they have no problem with their man going to strip clubs, but it doesn't matter, because again, men in love don't frequent strip clubs. Men who are in love want to spend time with their woman, watching a movie, making dinner together, making love and just being close in general, not spending multiple hours throwing singles at half-naked women. If your man is frequenting strip clubs then he's not in love with you.

55

A MAN WILL ONLY DO WHAT YOU LET HIM GET AWAY WITH. NOT TRUE

The reason this statement is not true, is that your man isn't treating you like crap, disregarding your feelings or cheating on you because you're letting him get away with it. He's treating you this way because he's not in love with you. It's not as if a man knows he's in love with you, but at the same time wants to see how far he can push the boundaries or see what he can get away with, it doesn't work that way.

If your man's in love with you he's never going to try to be sneaky or have anything to hide. He's this way because he doesn't respect you and doesn't care if he loses you as a result. He's going to do his dirt regardless whether you like it or not or whether you think you're letting him get away with it or not. When you take a stance or give him an ultimatum about his extra activities outside of the house, the only thing that means to him is he has to come up with new ways to be sneakier with his dirty deeds. For instance, if you argue that he's staying out too late, that doesn't mean that he'll stop the activities that's keeping him out late, it just means that he'll have to come up with new ways to appease you and keep doing his dirt on the side.

I COULD GO ON ALL DAY

The list goes on and on to physical abuse, lying, even using you for your money. But you get the idea. Remember, he's not doing his dirty deeds because you're letting him get away with them, he's doing these fucked up deeds because he wants to and will continue his fucked up ways regardless if you think you're letting him get away with them or not. If he can't fuck you over one way, he'll try another. Walk away!

56

IF HE'S RESPECTFUL TO HIS MOTHER, HE'LL BE RESPECTFUL TO HIS WOMAN. WRONG!

Most men, by nature, are good to their mothers and are momma's boys, and want their mothers to be well taken care of and happy.

As men we fantasize and have thoughts about wanting to surprise our mothers by buying her a house someday, sending her on expensive cruises and showering her with the best. We know our mothers love us unconditionally, even when we were unappreciative hard-headed, badass teenage boys causing her stress and grief.

Still, mother was always there to help us when we were in need, nurtured us when we were crying and took care of us when we were sick. She was always mom. The one person in the world we as guys know we can always count on for security. The older we get the instinct to want to be good to and appreciate our mothers begins to manifest. Now, having said all of that let's get on with the chapter.

IT JUST MEANS HE'S GOOD TO HIS MOTHER

I have heard so many women say, "If a man is good and respectful to his mother, he'll be good and respectful to his woman," wrong! The reality is it just means he's good to his mother. A man treats his mother like a queen who can do no wrong, and at the same time will turn around and be unappreciative and disregard you as his woman. The reason he does this is because, now say it with me, he's not in love with you! If your man treats you good it's because he wants to and is in love with you. It won't have anything to do with his relationship with his mother. Even if he's good to the both of you and treats you both like queens there's still no connection. It just means he's good to both of you.

Long short, a man's relationship with his mother never has and never will have anything to do with how he treats his woman.

The woman who raised him and the woman who he's sleeping with are two different entities in his mind. One entity is always worthy of his respect and admiration, and the other entity is disposable and replaceable. After all, he only has one mom, but he can always go to any club on a Saturday night and get another one of you, right?

MOM FOR A PROM DATE

There's a guy I know named Chris, who loves and thinks the world of his mom, so much so he took his mom to his senior prom as his date. All the girls at the prom thought this was such a sweet and beautiful gesture to his mother and showed a more in-depth insight into his true nature and character, so they thought. One girl in particular, Lisa, who inspired this chapter, thought that him taken his mom to the prom was so sweet, that the very next day she asked him out on a date. Her exact words to me were, "I asked him out because I know if a man is good and respectful to his mother, he'll be good and respectful to his woman."

Well, unfortunately for her, my tell-all book about men wasn't written at that time, and she didn't get the opportunity to benefit from my male expertise and save herself a lot of heartache. Moving on. Two years later, they married and started their wonderful life together as a young couple and Lisa couldn't have been happier with her new husband, "Who's so good to his mother," until one day the reality set in and she learned the terrible truth about her husband. He had been cheating on her since the first day they started going out. He had many girlfriends and been taking them to hotels and even in their bed while she was at work. To make matters worse, she would also learn that he was selling drugs, crack cocaine to be exact.

Lisa was devastated and heartbroken. Did it matter that he was getting some pussy on the side or that he was making extra money as a crack cocaine dealer? No. Because if you think about it, he was always good to his mother, right?

In the end she divorced him and she learned the hard way that just because a man's good and respectful to his mother doesn't always mean that he'll be good and respectful to his woman.

57

CHEATING ON YOU WITH HIS FRIENDS

Is your man spending more of his free time with his friends than you? Yes, every guy needs his time to spend with his buddy's. After all, it's perfectly healthy in a relationship for two people to give each other space and to hang out with their friends and have some form of a social life outside of each other. However, in a year's period of time, if he has clocked more of his free hours with his buddy's instead of you, it means he's no longer interested, he wants to get away, he needs an escape, and he's longing to gain his independence back. He might not even be mad at you or anything like that, but it does mean that you're no longer his best friend and he's fallen out of love with you, and that's if he even regarded you in that way in the first place.

A MAN IN LOVE WANTS TO SPEND TIME WITH HIS WOMAN

As much as we love hanging out with our boys whether it be at the bar, the game, watching the game on TV or whatever, when we're in love we never forget that our woman is our best friend and wanting to hang out and spend time with her is important to us. Not because it's our duty, but because we want to. We look forward to going to new places and experiencing something fun and exciting with her. For instance, when a new movie is coming out that you're both looking forward to seeing, going hiking or jogging together, going to that new restaurant or club that just opened up, working on a fun house project, watching TV or playing video games together at home. Whatever it may be, a man in love is not going to spend more time with his friends than the woman he loves.

DON'T TRY TO FIX THE PROBLEM

Don't waste your time trying to fix the problem by planning a date night or days you two can spend together or even talking to him about it, because if he wanted to spend time with you he would without you having to initiate it or plan for it.

He's not spending time with you because he doesn't want to and by you trying to fix the problem by creating situations for you two to be in together will only make him more annoyed and he'll start to feel inconvenienced. Then he's going to resent you for boxing him into a corner and making him do something he doesn't want to do. Walk away!

58

STOP FIGHTING OVER A MAN

If you're going to fight the other woman that you think your man is cheating on you with then you've already lost before the first punch is thrown and the first wad of hair is pulled out. There's a difference between fighting for your man and fighting over him. I'll explain below.

FIGHTING FOR YOUR MAN

Fighting for your man means when you and your man are out at the club and your man accidentally bumps into a woman and spills her drink. Then she decides to get all up in your man's face and cuss him out. If you decide to beat her to the floor that's considered fighting for your man, men are OK with that, because he recognizes that as you standing up for him and after all he can't hit a woman right?

In most cases a guy thinks that's hot and gets turned on by the fact that you stood up for him and might want to take you into the bathroom or in the car for a quickie afterwards. Of course a real man tries to defuse the situation before it escalates into a catfight, because after all, no man in love wants his woman fighting.

FIGHTING OVER YOUR MAN

Fighting over your man means when you and your man are out at the club, you see that bitch Leslie on the dance floor, and you know she likes your man. You also know that they had a conversation earlier that week when they ran into each other at the car wash. So, because of this you decide that you're going to confront her when she walks out into the parking lot. Once outside, you get in her face and accuse her of pushing up on your man and all. Then the next thing you know, hair extensions, earrings and ripped pieces of clothing are scattered all over the ground. The problem with this attitude is the very man you're fighting over will eventually walk away from you.

This is why, when you're fighting over a man you're making such asses of yourselves. Unless you're a troublemaker who's attracted to and always trying to start drama there is no reason for you to be fighting another woman over your man. If he is cheating with her, it's not as if you fighting her is going to make him develop feelings for you or make his feelings for you grow stronger, or make him realize that you're the better candidate just because you decided to attack and exchange fists with the other woman. It doesn't work that way. In fact it's the opposite effect. Even if he's not cheating, it turns a man off when a woman tries to fight another woman out of jealousy. Sure, sometimes it's funny, and he'll get to brag to his boys about how two girls were fighting over him, but to a man it's unattractive and not ladylike at all. Because for a man to fall in love with a lady, you first have to act like a lady. Also, when you're fighting over a man it shows you in a light as being an unstable woman who can't control herself or her emotions, and no man wants to be in a relationship with a woman like that. So, if you have legitimate proof that your man is cheating on you, then act like a lady and walk away.

WHY ARE YOU MAD AT THE OTHER WOMAN? SHE HAS NO OBLIGATION TO YOU

Stop directing your anger at the other woman who's currently sleeping with your man, because she has no obligation to you. She's not the one who's supposed to be in a relationship with you. She's not the one who said "I love you," and she's not the one who got you pregnant. Your man is obligated to you, your man is supposed to be in a relationship with you, your man is the one who said "I love you," and your man is the one who got you pregnant. Remember, a woman can't take your man from you, he has to volunteer to go.

Your man is the problem, not the other woman he's screwing. Actually, if you know there is another woman and you're still trying to fight for a man who's cheating on you then you're the problem. It's time to take accountability and face the reality that your man is not in love with you, he's not even in love with the other woman, you're both just something to do for right now.

I remember watching the TV show, "Caught on Camera," and they were showing video footage of two women in their early twenties fighting over a man. These two girls were beating the crap out of each other and were both covered in blood. Do you know after all of that fighting, bloodshed and ripped out hair, the commentator announced that the man that they were fighting over ended up not dating either of those women, but left both of them for someone else. Those two women should feel like the biggest dumbasses in the world.

For any woman fighting over a man you can for sure expect the same results, more than likely your man will kick you and the other woman to the curb when he's done with the both of you.

IN CLOSING

When it comes to your man and the other woman, don't get even, get on with your life. Don't stalk them, go driving by their houses, checking their social media pages and calling and hanging up from different numbers. Like a band-aid rip it off and be done.

Since we're on the subject, don't vandalize their cars or property either. Remember, you're not losing a man when you've found out he's been cheating, you're getting rid of dead weight. It might hurt in the beginning, but a couple of years from now your life will be so much better for having dropped his ass! However, what you don't need is to rid yourself of him but gain an expensive lawsuit in the process. You got bills to pay like we all do, and I'm sure you don't need to add a $5000.00 vandalizing bill to them. Be smart, not emotional.

59

S.T.D. CHECK UP. I'LL GO NEXT WEEK, OR MAYBE NEXT MONTH

I know a woman who called me one morning crying about how her man gave her an STD. Later that same night she told me that she was stopping at a restaurant to bring him his favorite dinner. Some women don't know when to walk away, even if they get an STD.

HE'D RATHER CARRY THE DISEASE THAN CONFRONT IT

Guys are experts at carrying a disease for long periods. Guys walk around for months with all kinds of itching and burning sensations coming from their penis areas just to avoid having to face the ordeal of going to the clinic. They know there's a problem down there and recognize the symptoms because chances are they've had them before, but still they keep telling themselves that they'll deal with it in a couple of days or next week. Then it turns into two weeks, three weeks, a month and then two months. All the while they're still having sex with you or with other women. Guys are just selfish in that way. They know that they're burning and itching but they still want to put it inside of you. Some guys think that if they wear a condom that the woman won't get what they got. Other guys don't even care and go bare and feel that, "If she gets burnt then it's her problem now. What's the big deal? She'll just have to go to the doctor and get a prescription to clear it up. But I still need to get mine!"

You'll usually find this type of behavior with single guys because single guys don't have as many responsibilities as men who are married or in relationships.

They don't have to answer to a woman, meaning they don't have to worry about burning their wife or girlfriend. So they'll sleep with two or three different women say in a six week period while burning and itching without missing a beat or fear of consequences. They usually don't care if they burn a woman or how it affects her. Their mindset is, "Oh well, shit happens."

However, men who are married or in relationships who cheat for the most part usually deal with the problem in a reasonable amount of time because they don't want to run the risk of giving what they caught to their main woman. Remember, I said, for the most part, but not always.

Why guys carry their disease around as opposed to just getting it cleared up and taken care of immediately is not a big mystery. They're guys and immature, bottom line. No matter how bad their symptoms are, guys avoid getting checked out to the very last minute. You have to be careful who you lie with because you might get more than an orgasm.

WE ARE LIARS!

All of my female friends and associates who have a friend with benefits situation are very delusional about why their arrangement with their booty call is so different and unique. They all say the same thing, "We're real and honest with each other, and there's no secrets."

"No secrets?" If they only knew. So let's break down the difference between what they and most of you women think is going on with the booty call guys in your lives.

1. WHAT A WOMAN SAYS: "We're honest and upfront with each other. There's no secrets."

THE REALITY IS: No, he's not honest and upfront with you. He's only telling you what you want to hear, fact! When it comes to getting a piece of ass men don't care about honesty. They'll tell you whatever you want to hear and deal with the consequences later.

2. WHAT A WOMAN SAYS: "He tells me about every other woman he sleeps with."

THE REALITY IS: No, he doesn't tell you about every woman he sleeps with. He'll tell you enough to make himself seem genuine and sincere, but other than that if he says that he's only sleeping with two other women, then you can add three more to that count. That's three more chances that you'll catch something.

3. WHAT A WOMAN SAYS: "He always wears condoms with the other women."

THE REALITY IS: When a man tells you that he always wears a condom with those other women he's lying! No questions asked. He's only using condoms fifty percent of the time, and now you get to carry the other woman's disease.

4. WHAT A WOMAN SAYS: "He tells me he goes to the clinic and gets checked out once a month."

THE REALITY IS: Men avoid the clinic like they do paying child support. Unless a man is bringing you a documented paper that gives him a clean bill of health, always assume he has something.

STOP BEING STUPID!

It's almost as if you women want to believe that besides you he has other women who he sleeps with, but out of all of them you're unique and his main one. He's not always a hundred percent with them, but with you he always keeps it real.

Let me say this loud and upfront, MEN ARE LIARS! We might be stupid, but we know when and how to come off as real and sincere. We know how to act like we have no reason to lie to you, especially when it comes to sex. We don't care how much we like you as a person, if we've known each other for years or even think that you are a little special, because when it comes to sex men will lie to get some, and guys don't care if you catch a disease in the process. So keep that in mind next time you text him at 1:00 a.m. talkin bout "Whatcha doin?" He's scratching his dick that's what he's doing.

60

THERE'S NO SUCH THING AS A BAD BOY

That's right. There is no such thing as a bad boy. It doesn't exist. Your mind is just working overtime trying to see things in him that aren't there. What you perceive as the bad boy is nothing more than an illusion that you've created about this guy in your head — a fantasy. Whatever your attraction is for this guy based on the fictional bad boy concept, whether it be excitement, adventure, indifference, coolness, confidence, unpredictability, is all just a temporary illusion.

GIRLS JUST WANT TO HAVE FUN!

1. He's so spontaneous.
2. He likes to jump in his car and drive to another city for no reason.
3. He likes to go skinny-dipping in the middle of the night.
4. I love going bar and club hopping with him.
5. He knows how to let loose and have a good time.
6. He's so real and down to earth; he farts and burps when he wants to. It's gross but funny at the same time.
7. When he walks into a room, everybody lights up and wants to be around him.
8. He makes me want to try new things that I've never done before.

Girls just want to have fun! Yea, I get it, he can be the funny, Mr. easy-going, life of the party, spontaneous attitude, anything goes, adventurous, not scared to get his nails dirty, get his feet wet, thinks outside of the box, and makes you forget all about your daily rut, guy. Well, who gives a shit? The bottom line is how does he treat you? That's all that matters, because fun and spontaneity doesn't equal a great guy.

Let me ask you a question, does he long for you throughout his day? Does he anticipate your phone call or text? Are you the first and last thing he thinks about when he wakes up and goes to bed? Does he want to be your protector and hero? Then again, if he were that attentive toward you, you probably wouldn't be all that hung up over him or even find him that appealing in the first place, right? If he were that much of an attentive, caring person, he'd probably be too boring for you, am I correct? After all, bad boys aren't supposed to care or show any real concern for your well-being, right? No, instead you're going to sit there and put some guy on a pedestal, give him the keys to your heart and emotions just because he's "spontaneous" and "knows how to have a good time?" Now, don't get me wrong, I'm not suggesting that you become involved with a man who doesn't even know how to laugh at himself, or knows how to jump in the water headfirst from time to time. I'm just saying stop giving a guy more credit than what he's worth just because he knows how to entertain you or does things that appeal to your adventurous side. It doesn't mean he's special or worthy of your heart and body, it just means in those particular areas he's spontaneous. I have plenty of guy friends who fit all of the above examples who are in relationships and show their women a good time, but the problem is they're emotionally unattached to these women. They're never going to want to be in fulfilling relationships with these women, why? Because these women don't measure up in some way shape or form in their eyes. They're just something to do for right now, yet these women think that these "bad boy" friends of mine are just so fun to be around.

If you can find a guy who fits all of these fun characteristics and he's treating you like a queen, then more power to you. However, if you're dating, in a relationship or married to your fun and spontaneous guy, who makes you forget all about your daily rut, regardless of how much fun and out the box he is, if he's not longing for you, and if you're not the core of his desire, then you're just setting yourself up for a fall. Do not substitute cheap thrills and entertainment for emotional substance.

WELL, WHO CARES? I'M HAVING FUN AND
MY HEART WANTS WHAT IT WANTS

And Meth addicts want meth and to get high every day, what's your point? Let me ask you a question. Don't you feel ridiculous wanting someone who doesn't want you back? "Yea, I'm not the core of his desire, but at least I have fun when I'm with him," duh. At what point does common sense and intelligence take over your brain? Remember when I said, "You women give us men way too much credit?" Maybe you should go back and read that chapter again.

HE'S SO MYSTERIOUS AND DANGEROUS.
THERE'S SOMETHING ABOUT HIM

No, there's nothing about him, except the illusions that you're creating in your mind. I had a friend who once told me that she had a crush on a guy who was a drummer in a local rock band. She said she found it hot that even though he was a nice guy he had a hint of danger to him because he was in a band and covered in tattoos.

This is an example of a female's imagination running away with her. Sure, he might be a nice guy, but no, just because he's a drummer in a rock band that doesn't mean he's a little dangerous. It just means he beats on tom-toms and a snare drum in a group of musicians that include four or five other people. As far as his tattoos are concerned, again, it doesn't make him dangerous; it just means he paid someone with an electric needle a few hundred dollars to put ink all over his body. My Grandmother has five tattoos, but that hardly makes her a bad girl or a tough momma. What's happening here is that the male is creating the illusion with this imagery, and the female's imagination is doing the rest.

HE'S SUCH A DARK AND TORTURED SOUL. THAT'S SO SEXY!

OK? In reality, he's just confused, insecure and trying to find an identity or belief system to embrace. Deep down he's dying for someone to tell him who he is and what to believe. In a few years he'll try to be someone else.

HE'S SUCH A DEEP THINKER. HE'S SO ATTUNE. HE HAS A THIRD EYE

Oh yes, the woman who wants a man who challenges her mentally. His mind works on a higher level, and he has insight that the rest of us simpletons can only hope to acquire. Let me guess, he makes you think and makes you want to be a better person? And there's nothing wrong with that, but let me ask you, HOW DOES HE TREAT YOU?

HE'S SO CONFIDENT

There is no such thing as a confident man, like there is no such thing as a confident woman. Either can't exist. As people, there are just some areas in our character that we're confident in and other areas where we're insecure. Even that changes back and forth as we get older and life hits us hard from different angles. However, nine times out of ten when a woman is attracted to a man's "confidence," that she perceives as strength, what she's really responding to is his arrogance. They're two different things.

The facts are, what women usually think makes a man strong/confident, mentally and emotionally are wrong. A man displays a specific type of arrogant behavior and a woman thinks that it means **A** when it really means **B**. You've conditioned yourself to believe that the wrong things means a man has inner strength.

Many women think arrogant/cocky equals emotional strength and all the other attributes that come with it. When in reality, arrogant and cocky actually means he's weak, mentally and emotionally un-evolved. Moreover, they let this emotionally weak man take charge because, "He's such a take-charge kind of guy," when in reality, he has no clue what the fuck he's doing. It's the blind leading the blind. This is another example of you women giving us way too much credit.

Think of it this way. There are men out there who are great street fighters. Those who really know how to fight and have real inner strength don't make it a point to go around showing off or bragging about their fighting talent. They're calm, subtle, but when the time comes for action they're like a stick of dynamite that goes off and does some real damage.

Then you have those who aren't great street fighters or have minimum ability, but they overcompensate by barking the loudest, put on a big show, pick on someone smaller. But when the time for action comes they either quiver into a corner or end up getting knocked out.

But, let's turn it around for a moment. He might be a great street fighter who has knocked out over a hundred men in his time. However, outward strength still doesn't equal inner strength, and inner strength is the real substance.

The bottom line is, men with real inner strength don't have to walk around holding a sign advertising their gifts, looking for attention or feel the need to be continuously validated, and that's the difference.

ALPHA MALE MYTH

Alpha males are like Bigfoot, there are so many people who've claimed to have seen one but the data or video footage is unclear. Bottom line is they don't exist. I know you know of a group of guys, maybe your boyfriend or associates, and they all seem to gravitate toward one guy in the group who seems to be the leader or the deciding voice. The thing is, guys can respond to other guys the way females do, guys can also be drawn to another guy's "Arrogance" and "strength," in a, 'I wish I were more like him and had what he has,' way. He has that "confidence" they wish they had. So they live vicariously threw him so to speak and they let him take charge and lead the group.

But this so-called, "Alpha Male," is just as insecure unsure and weak as they are. The difference is, his shortcomings are just in different areas. He's better at masking them, and whatever "confident vibe" he's putting out there that they're responding to, if they like what he's selling he'll keep giving it to them to be the ring leader.

HIS ACCENT/DEEP VOICE IS SEXY!

I remember back in the day when I was living in Arizona; there was a family of brothers. I can't remember where they were from but they had very distinct accents. As a result, every woman in the city was throwing themselves at them. These guys had sex coming at them from all directions. It wasn't that they were that great looking, they weren't bad looking, but it wasn't that serious. They just had accents that the women couldn't resist. Every time a female friend or acquaintance of mine would talk about one of them they always said the same thing, "Their accents are so hot!" All of these women were spreading their legs for them just because of the way they talked?

Ladies, his accent is just that, an accent. His deep voice is just that, a deep voice. Yes, I get you find them sexy, we all have our things that turn us on and draw us to the opposite sex. The reality is, it has nothing to do with his inner strength, character, personality, or even if he's going to be a good man to you. It just means he talks a certain way. Now, if you want to buy into the illusion that him having a deep voice or accent means that he's sexy, a great lover, or even romantic, you have that option. But at the end of the day, it's just the way he talks, period. It's not designed to enhance the sex, your life, or relationship.

But by all means have at it. Duh?

HE'S SO FUNNY AND CHARISMATIC

I know sometimes women say, "I don't care if he doesn't have much money, if he can make me laugh, that's what's important." I say, I don't care if he can make you laugh till you start shooting fireworks out cha ass! Bottom line, how does he treat you? I have a lot of friends that are funny, entertaining guys. They make their women die laughing, and they're also cheating on them.

HE'S SO DRIVEN AND AMBITIOUS

Nothing wrong with being goal orientated. I can understand how that can be an appealing quality to a woman, but again, how does he treat you?

CREATING ILLUSIONS IN YOUR MIND
INSTEAD OF SEEING IT FOR WHAT IT IS

I remember when the rapper 50 Cent first came on the hip-hop scene and all the girls were talking about how sexy it was that he was shot and hit by nine bullets in a feud and didn't die. I suppose in their heads this made him some kind of Robo Brotha that even bullets couldn't penetrate and bring down, and that just made him even more appealing to thousands of women around the world and so on. Even my girlfriend was talking about how hot it was that nine bullets couldn't stop him.

Now, don't get me wrong, I think 50 Cent is a great artist and I have nothing bad to say about him or his music. And that's awesome and a blessing that he survived the attack. But the reality of that situation was, no, he isn't a Robo Brotha, and him being hit by nine bullets and surviving wasn't designed to make him more appealing or desirable. It just means that the nine bullets that hit him didn't hit any major arteries that could have caused a fatality. This is a small example of how females create illusions and fantasies and get carried away with them.

I LOVE THE BAD BOY GANGSTAS

I had a friend tell me this once, and she's going to be pissed that I mentioned this, so I'll keep her name out of this. My white female friend once told me, when she was in her mid-late teens, she thought it was so hot and sexy when she saw "thugs" wearing du-rags, standing around and drinking their 40 ounces. Well, OK, in her imagination that was working overtime she created an image that these guys were so sexy, bad boys to be exact. Her thoughts about these "bad boys" probably went something like this.

Wow! Look at those guys. They act as if they don't have a care in the world. They stand on the corner, or the parking lot of the club drinking their malt liquor and cracking inside jokes that only they understand.

What's even hotter is their pants are pulled down, revealing their buttocks that are covered by loose-fitting boxer shorts.

Oh, and those tattoos on their arms of their dead homies names, or the names of the street or gang they're from adds to the excitement and mystery.

Oh, and the way they give each other pounds and hugs lets me know that they're down for theirs and have each other's backs.

Look! The bad boy gangsta on the right has a chain in his hand connected to a vicious Pit bull. Yeah, the Pit bull will attack and devour anybody who gets too close to it, but his bad-boy gangsta master is the only one who can tame it and tell it what to do.

Oh wait, one of them is talking on his phone. I don't know who it is, but I'm sure that it's a very important call by someone who only a select few can talk to, and he's one of the few elite who can. He must be special.

Wait a minute, a car just pulled up next to them. One of them is walking up to it. Now he's talking into the window. Wow, I bet they're having an in-depth discussion about a serious drug deal that's going to go down soon, involving a lot of money. But, he doesn't care about the consequences because he's keeping it real, a soldier, and he has to get his!

Oh listen, one of them is talking about his baby's momma. That's so hot that he has someone to call his baby's momma. She must have been lucky to have his baby. I'm sure she realizes that others know that she's fortunate to have his seed. It must be awesome when he comes to the house to drop off money or baby supplies. Sure, he can't stay long because he has important business and people to get back to, and even though he doesn't spend time with his baby he still loves his child. Besides, his baby's momma probably nags and trips on him too much. She just doesn't understand him, that's why he can't be with her. Things would be different if I was with him and was his girl. I wouldn't trip when he was out late. I know he's taking care of business and I'm not worried about the other girls because he would have a good woman at home. I would watch and spend time with his baby and be a better mother to his child than the baby's real mother ever could.

Oh, and even though he keeps a lot of money and drugs in the house, he trusts me not to touch it. If the police ever questioned me about him or his activities, I would deny and not say anything. My bad boy drug-dealing boyfriend would love and appreciate me more for that.

Am I close enough girls? I could see how a young female in her mid-late teens could find this attractive and appealing, **duh**? Yes, the female mind can create all kinds of illusions when it comes to men and how they perceive them. Right now, let's break down this particular bad boy scenario brick by brick and reveal it for what it really is.

BRICK BY BRICK

1. They act as if they don't have a care in the world because they don't know anything else or motivated about anything else.
2. They hang out at the club/parking lot because they don't have anywhere else constructive to be, literally.
3. They really can't handle the beer and alcohol they're drinking, and chances are they'll be throwing it up before the end of the night or bitching that they don't feel so good.
4. The inside jokes they're telling each other aren't that funny, are pretty stupid, and each one who told a joke is laughing harder than his boys listening.
5. Their pants are pulled down to the bottom of their asses because even though it's uncomfortable as hell to walk like this, they see all of their other friends doing it. So being the followers that they are, they have to do it too. The keyword is "Followers."
6. When they got their tattoos put on, they cried and whined the whole time and even considered not finishing the job.
7. Even though they give each other pounds, hugs and act like they got each other's backs, truth be told, if anyone of them were to get arrested for a drug charge, they would gladly cut a deal with the Feds and snitch on one of their "homies" to save their own asses.
8. The vicious Pit bull that the bad-boy gangsta is holding on to is more than likely scared of its own shadow, recently lost a dog fight its owner put' em in and even though it looks like a scary dog, it's just for show. The owner thinks having a scary-looking dog makes him look tougher.
9. The person he's talking to on his phone isn't anybody important; in fact, it's just some girl he's been trying to hook up with who keeps giving him the runaround.

10. The person he's talking to in the car that pulled up next to them is someone he owes money to and he's asking for an extension.

11. His baby's momma is just as pathetic as he is for ever having slept with him and bringing a child into the world with such an immature, no goal orientated, "keeping it real" dumb ass! Yeah, she's really lucky and fortunate.

12. Unfortunately the baby that he never spends time with that he calls his "Little soldier" or "little man" or if it's a girl "his heart" will more than likely grow up with some psychological issues, all because mommy had to screw a "bad boy" and end up with a father who only calls or writes him/her when he's in prison. However, the child is probably better off without having a dumbass for a daddy in his/her life.

13. "His baby's momma doesn't understand him, but things would be different if you two were together?" Yeah right, you would be in the same situation his baby's momma is in right now. He wouldn't be giving you any money and wouldn't visit you or your imaginary psychologically messed up child you laid down and had together. The only thing that would be different is the baby's momma's not putting up with his immature little boy ass, you would.

HE ACTS LIKE HE DOESN'T CARE. I FIND THAT SEXY. IT MAKES ME WANT HIM MORE

I wanted to come back and elaborate a little more on this concept. When I asked females, what exactly makes a guy a bad boy in their eyes, the most common response that I got was, "A bad boy is a guy who acts like he doesn't care."

Again, women tend to see things that aren't there. The truth is, what you want to think of as a guy who doesn't care just means he hasn't evolved in many areas of his character. There are plenty of men out there, who don't care about many things, but you're not running after these particular guys or calling them bad boys, why is that? Instead, you're running after a particular guy because you're attracted to him and you want to slap a, "He acts like he doesn't care," bad boy title on him to give him more appeal.

I know a woman who once said to me that the more her husband acts as if he doesn't care or wants her, the more it makes her want him, how sad is that? News flash, him acting like he doesn't care or wants you, in reality, isn't designed to make him more appealing or desirable. It just means he doesn't want you, period! Instead of praying to God to strengthen your relationship, go ask the Wizard to give you a brain.

As females get older they tend to outgrow the idea of the "bad boy," and after a lot of heartbreak and disappointments, they began to look at the "Bad boy," for what he is and not the fantasy they initially created in their heads. Eventually the illusion fades off, and then you're stuck with having to deal with the real person who, "doesn't care." By then, him acting like he doesn't care won't seem so appealing. In most cases it'll already be too late because you'll end up having a child with your bad boy and then you'll be stuck with that in common and with each other until one of you is deceased.

Sure, he doesn't support you emotionally, have a real future and won't be able to provide for you or the baby that you've had with him, but that's OK, because his, "I don't care," attitude will provide for you, and keep the heat on, and put food in the baby's mouth, right?

WELL WHO CARES IF IT'S NOT REAL. I STILL FIND HIS, "I DON'T CARE," ATTITUDE SEXY AND APPEALING

Now, let's be clear, if wanting to believe that this guy is so appealing because he gives off the bad boy vibe or image that he doesn't care and you're drawn to that, and there's something inside the female psyche that responds to that behavior from men, even if you know it's an illusion, is not a bad thing. After all most of our attractions aren't based on factuality in the first place. Most of our attractions are based a little bit on fantasy and seeing things in the opposite sex or other person that aren't there. We can all agree with that, right?

The question is, how much of yourself and your emotions are you willing to invest into the illusion until you realize that you need to be in a relationship with a little more substance and not based on fantasy, image and idealism. In the end you have to take accountability for the outcome.

I CAN CHANGE HIM

It's not your job to change a man regardless of what his issues are. But let's go with that idea for a moment. You think you can, "change him," or that he'll change for you. You can't even figure you out, or control your own emotions, but you think you're going to convince a man to submit and conform to become what you want him to be? When a woman says, "I can change him," what she's really thinking is, *eventually he'll come around.* I tell you what, I know at least twelve women in their forties who are still waiting for him to, "come around." If you want to invest another ten to fifteen years of your life waiting to see if he'll, "come around," all I can say is good luck with that.

HE HASN'T EVOLVED FROM A BOY TO A MAN

I remember when an ex-girlfriend of mine once said to me, the older I've gotten the more square I've become. She asked me, "What happened to the bad boy that I once knew?" OK, I guess from her perspective she probably had a point. I had changed a lot since I was in my late teens and early twenties. No, I don't steal cars or sell drugs anymore. I don't run the streets like I used to, or try to bed every woman I meet. Still, I had to clarify a few things with her. Not that there's anything wrong with being a square, but there's a big difference between a man being a square vs. a man who has matured and evolved emotionally. Yes, I have put away childish things and immature self-indulged ways of thinking. I definitely "care" more than ever. Because going through life acting like the world revolved around me and my fucked up way of thinking only backfired in a major way. It blew up in my face. As I got older I began to realize that there's a whole world outside of my ego and my imagination. It was time to grow up, mature and evolve, because as the male species if we're not evolving then we're just stuck on stupid. Behold, I give you the bad boy.

61

THERE ARE NO GOOD MEN OUT THERE

Nothing, and I mean nothing could be further from the truth. Society is overflowing with great guys who would love to appreciate you and treat you like a queen. Good men are a dime a dozen. The problem is we've conditioned ourselves to go after what we want instead of what we need.

STOP THINKING WITH RESTRICTIONS AND LIMITATIONS

Your chances of meeting a man who wants to treat you like a goddess would happen so much faster if you were willing to come outside of your little box and comfort zone. Who cares if he's not the same race as you, who cares if he's a little younger or older than you, who cares if he doesn't make as much money as you would like, who cares if he's going bald, who cares if he's a little overweight, who cares if he's a Dallas Cowboys fan and you're from Seattle? Who cares what your little differences are because they're not deciding factors on whether or not a man is going to be good to you and for you.

By putting these types of limitations on the men that you allow into your life, you limit yourself to the possibilities of you ever finding or being with someone who'll treat you the way you deserve.

TONYA

The smartest thing I ever heard a woman say about a man is, "God has already picked out a **GREAT** man for me. But, when I finally meet him, I know he's not going to be who I thought he would be."

When I was in my late teens, I had a friend named Tonya. Tonya was always dating the, "Bad boy" drug dealers, who had the flashy cars, wore the latest fashions and hung out at the coolest hot spots. She found these types of men appealing, sexy, hot, and desirable, so she made herself available to them.

The problem was she would call me almost every other night to complain and cry about the way her, "bad boy" drug-dealing boyfriends were treating her. They were always treating her like crap. They were verbally and physically abusive toward her and always disregarded her feelings. Of course, she didn't mind, because after all, she wanted these guys to like her and wanted their approval.

For the next few years Tonya continued to pursue these types of men and we eventually grew apart, until ten years later when I ran into her at the grocery store. After hugging and a little bit of catching up, she told me she was married to a great guy named Taylor and called her husband over to meet me. When I saw her husband I was a little shocked because he was nothing like the types of guys she used to date. He was short, very skinny, dorky and anything but a "Bad boy." He didn't look the part or fit the description. After he walked away, Tonya and I continued talking, and I couldn't help but to comment on her man, and I said, "He doesn't look like the type of guy that you used to date?" The response she gave to me was clearly from a woman who had evolved. She said, "I used to date those bad-boy drug dealers because I thought that they were hot and all that drug dealing stuff that they did was sexy and mysterious. I grew up. I began to realize that I never really wanted that type of a guy. All I ever wanted was for someone to treat me good and show me lots of attention, and you know what? Taylor treats me like a princess; I'm so blessed to have him."

It's great that Tonya found someone who loves her and wants to treat her like a princess. The point is, she would have never found Taylor if she hadn't come out of her little box and comfort zone.

I DON'T WANT TO SETTLE

I have another friend, Katelyn, who was in a similar situation where she too was being treated like crap by the man in her life, while at the same time another man was trying to court her. The guy courting her wasn't a bad looking guy, but he wasn't a great looking guy. Still, he was always attentive toward her, would send her flowers and take her out to nice dinners, and was always a gentleman to her. One time when she was working with the flu, he brought medicine and chicken noodle soup to her job because he cared; he was a great guy.

One day I asked her why she doesn't dump her idiot boyfriend who continuously treats her like the gum underneath his shoe, and date the guy who was courting her and treating her good. Do you know what her response was, "The reason I won't date him is because I don't want to settle." Her answer blew me away. Because I was her friend I had to give her brutal honesty, I said, "Let me get this straight, your boyfriend continuously treats you like crap, and you're still trying to hang on to him, while this other guy thinks the world of you and isn't afraid to show it. He shows you unselfish amounts of attention and you think choosing him would be settling? How could choosing someone who adores you and treats you like a queen over someone who treats you like car wax be settling? The truth is, Katelyn, he's the one that's settling." Do you know even as I write this book today, she's still with the same guy and he still treats her like shit?

I'M WAITING FOR SOMETHING BETTER

Let me save you the trouble. There's always going to be something better, always! Superficially that is. There's always going to be a guy with a hotter body, a hotter face, a bigger dick, a cooler car, a nicer house and who makes more money. But, none of that matters, because nothing and I mean nothing will ever be better than being with a man who loves and adores you for you. Don't learn this the hard way.

62

TREAT WOMEN LIKE SHIT AND THEY'LL BEG FOR MORE

If I had a son and he came to me one day and said, "Dad, I like a girl at school. What can I do to win her heart?" Honestly I'd be stumped. What could I say to him? Should I tell him A or B?

A. "Son, you should give her respect, treat her good and sincerely listen to her, and she'll melt in your arms."

B. "Unfortunately son, we live in a society where a lot of females only respond to men if they treat'em like crap. Not all, but they're a lot of them out there. So chances are to win her heart and make her want you, you'll have to disregard her feelings, show her very little respect, don't do what you say you're going to do, oh, and act like you don't care, and she'll make you the center of her world. Son, I didn't write the rule book for the dating game, I'm just trying to teach you the best way I know with the information and experiences that I've acquired over the years."

Again, I ask you, which advice should I give my son?

AGAIN, TREAT WOMEN LIKE SHIT, IT WORKS! I CAN VOUCH FOR IT

While I was coming up, I had females at my disposal around the clock. My phone rang at all hours of the night. If I wanted a piece of ass all I had to do was whistle. The point is, the more I treated females like shit and showed them I didn't care about them, the more they wanted me. Honestly, I felt like I could treat these women any way I wanted to and get away with it. They were just doormats waiting for me to wipe my feet on them. For the record I've never physically hurt a woman in my life. That I don't play.

I remember this fine ass sista that I was dating who let me get away with anything with her. I was becoming less and less attracted to her because she always let me use her and treat her like crap. I got to a point where I would try and see how far I could go before she got turned off. One night while lying in bed watching a movie, I wanted to put it to the test. We were spooning, and she was behind me. I let out the loudest hardest fart on her, and it smelled horrible. I was laughing my ass off, and you know what, all she did was smack me on the head, but she never moved out from behind me. A few minutes later she started holding me closer? All I could think was, *I continuously treat you like shit, I just covered you in shit fumes, and you're holding me closer? I have to get rid of this girl.* I had mastered the golden rule, "Treat women like shit or even shit on them, and they'll beg for more." She was just one out of many.

Now, I know you're thinking that I was wrong for treating her the way I did, and I should always treat women with respect and as a person. Also, women like a guy to be good to them, show them attention and let them know they're special, etc. OK, I hear you; we'll get to that point.

TINA

I worked at a Costco years ago and became very attracted to a co-worker, this sista named Tina. Everything about her was beautiful to me, her eyes, smile, lips and body. The highlight of my day was when she would come out of the office so I could get a glimpse of her. In my mind if I won her over, I would forsake every other woman in the world for her, and I meant it. As time went on I would make small talk with her and throw in a few jokes here and there, until one day I got the nerve to ask her out. It's funny how I spent years treating females like shit, but when it came to Tina I was a bubbling idiot.

We went to Tony Roma's and a movie. I was a complete gentleman, holding doors open for her, letting her order first, watching my mouth when I spoke, etc. As we ate, I was as flattering and sincere as I could be, after all, this was my future wife. Later, I let her pick the movie and it was horrible, but I smiled through the whole thing because it was what she wanted to watch. When it was over I dropped her off at her house and gave her a gentle hug and we parted ways. As I drove home I was already visualizing asking her out again. I was in love! What I didn't know was trying to win her heart over the next year wasn't going to be easy at all.

I PAID SOME DUES

As time went on, every time I asked her out, Tina always seemed to be busy or had other plans. Obviously she was blowing me off with a smile. After a couple of months I asked her friend who worked with us why Tina was acting this way with me and her response caught me off guard. She quoted Tina and said that Tina was blowing me off because, "I was too nice, and she's used to going out with guys who weren't good to her." *What the fuck does that even mean?* I thought. At that time I had never heard of a woman saying anything like that. I was good to Tina and really liked her. I was sincere in wanting to get to know her better and spend more time with her. And because of her I didn't want to be a player anymore. I knew in the first five minutes of meeting her I wanted to be with her. I decided not to read into what her friend said or let that stop me. I was serious about winning her heart, so I moved forward, with "my nice self."

As the months went on, I continued to pursue Tina. She was starting to give me hints that she might like me a little bit but nothing too strong. Having to pursue a standoffish woman was new territory for me. I wasn't used to it and didn't know what to do or how to handle it. So instead of backing off and playing it cool, I turned the heat up more. I would do things like put cards on her windshield, have single roses sent to her at work, bring her breakfast and lunch, have long talks with her on the phone when she was having family problems. One time on her birthday, I even baked her favorite kind of cake and brought it and her favorite ice cream to work and surprised her in the parking lot with them. I even went as far as recording a song for her in the studio and gave it to her. She loved it. Even her parents were impressed by the attention I was giving her. However, after a year of this, she was still showing no interest in me other than thinking that I was just a really sweet, "nice guy." Again, this was the first time in my life that I had seriously pursued a woman while getting shot down repeatedly.

I was confused? *I thought women wanted to be romanced and swept off of their feet?* This was what all my female friends were telling me they wanted, a guy to do sweet romantic things for them. This is what women on TV said they wanted, "a romantic guy." So why wasn't it working with Tina? And how come the more I tried to be her Prince Charming the more she put me in the friend zone? We didn't call it the friend zone back then of course, but I was starting to feel like nothing I did was ever going to win her over.

FUCK IT!

After a whole year she agreed to go out on another date with me again. We made plans to go to the movies. To this day I remember being in my room and thinking to myself about what my next step with her would be. I thought, *No matter how good I am to her she just doesn't want me. I spend money, I'm sincere, I'm always doing romantic things and nothing seems to work. I keep coming up short?* That's when the light bulb came on over my head. I had a moment of clarity. The idea had come to me and it was so obvious that if it were a snake it would've bitten me. I now knew what I had to do to win her over. I thought to myself, *I'm gonna do somethin' different tonight. I'm gonna purposely treat her like shit and act like I don't give a damn!*

From the time I arrived at her house I was a complete asshole. I didn't give a fuck. But it was all an act. Instead of going to the door like last time I blew my horn. I didn't even get out to open her door for her. When she got to my car the first thing that came out of my mouth was, "Check the bottom of your shoes before you get in my car. I don't want no dirt and shit in here." She was taken back, but she did what I asked. I didn't acknowledge her and was quiet during the whole ride unless I was singing with the radio. Noticing my strange demeanor she asked me if anything was wrong and I said, "Nah, I'm cool."

When we arrived at the theatre, I got out of the car and continued to be silent. I started walking toward the theatre door, staying at least four steps in front of her. She hurried to keep up with me. Then I opened the theatre door but didn't hold it open for her, she gave me another confused look. I still didn't talk to her. When we arrived at the ticket counter I told the man two tickets and when he told me the price, I sucked my teeth, looked at her and said, "Well I guess I'm paying for this?" She said that she would pay for the tickets and quickly started digging in her purse. I just handed the man the money and said, "Whateva?"

When we got to the snack counter I ordered for me first and told her in a rude tone, "If you want something get it now because I'm not coming back out here later." I made it a point to sound extra rude. When I said that, even I thought that my tone of voice was so rude that she would probably tell me, "Screw you!" and to just take her back home. Instead, she did two things that shocked me.

1. As we were leaving the snack counter, she offered to carry my soda.
2. She wrapped her other arm around mine and held me close to her.

Wow, treating her like shit is really working, I thought.

When we sat down in the theatre, I purposely began talking all kinds of shit — cracking jokes, shooting my mouth off like I didn't give a fuck about anything. In the entire year I knew her I had never spoken around her in this way or seen her laugh, not even when I would be funny at work. However, on that night while I was, "being funny" and talking all kinds of garbage, she was laughing like everything I was saying was the funniest shit she had ever heard in her life. She kept her arm around me the whole time. A half-hour into the movie I got a third shocker from her, she leaned over and kissed me on the cheek. Her change of attitude blew me away. For the first time I knew I had her.

Still playing it cool and acting like I didn't give a fuck I drove her back home. She talked my ear off the whole ride. All of a sudden she had a new sense of enthusiasm for me. When we arrived at her house she asked me to come in so she could show me the inside, but I said I had to get going. Still giving her attitude, I said, "Come on close my door, it's freezing!" She looked disappointed that I turned her down. Then she leaned in to kiss me, and I pulled back and said, "Girl we just ate all of that junk food and we haven't even brushed our teeth. I'm good." She was stunned. I was rejecting her now. She smiled at me and asked me to call her when I got home. I told her maybe and drove off.

I had succeeded! I had finally got her right where I wanted her. My plan to win her over by treating her like shit had worked, or did it?

You might think at this point that I would have been on cloud nine, but to be honest, while driving home, I was a little sad and disappointed about how the date went. I reflected on all the time that I spent courting her. I had spent all this time trying to win this woman's heart and affections by treating her like a queen, and she rejected and shot me down every step of the way. But, in one night I treated her like shit, and she was all over me. *That's pretty sad for her.* When I finished that thought, it was that very moment that I had realized that I had lost all attraction toward her. I thought, *How could I possibly be attracted to a woman who didn't respond to me when I came at her in realness. But, when I played games and treated her like shit, now all of a sudden she wants me?* It was a major turn off.

The following time we were employed together I was always kind to her. And even though she made attempts to go out with me again, I was always, "too busy."

BUT WHY WAS I NOW TURNED OFF FROM TINA?

Because it showed me either two things were happening.

1. By rewarding my rude, obnoxious behavior with affection and kisses, it possibly revealed her emotional immaturity.
2. Or, maybe she was the type of girl who was attracted to guys who acted like assholes because she found their false confidence and arrogance sexy and appealing? Either way, it was a turnoff.

Now, you might be thinking that her friend already told me that in the beginning, "I was too nice," so this shouldn't have come as a surprise to me when I started acting like a "bad boy" that Tina responded to my rude disregarding behavior, right?

However, here's the difference. I had no problem if Tina had low self-esteem, if her confidence was a little shaken from past heartaches and disappointments, or if she was scared to get involved with a guy who was, "too nice" because that made her skeptical of his intentions. If that were the case, I wouldn't have pushed her away because of that. That's called being human, and as her man or potential man, I'm not going to exploit her low self-esteem or take advantage of that. Instead, I'm going to do things to lift her confidence, encourage her, and remind her daily that she's special.

What caused me to push her away was because, after I showed her what an asshole I could be, even though I was acting, she could've only responded in two ways, immediately kick me to the curb, or become attracted to me.

If she would've immediately kicked me to the curb for treating her that way, I would've still been attracted to and respected her, why? Because even though her self-esteem was low, she would've still known that she deserved better than to be treated like that and walked away.

Because she responded to my negative behavior with such admiration and affection, it showed me she still had some growing and evolving to do. So that equals no attraction. How could I or any man possibly be drawn or attracted to a woman who responds positively to being treated like shit? I can be her friend and respect her as a person, but the romantic interest could never be. She showed me where her mind was at, revealed her emotional immaturity and not to waste any more of my time pursuing this woman on a romantic level.

LET THIS BE A LESSON TO YOU

Think about it like this, have you ever had a man in your life that you continuously used, cheated on and treated like complete shit? But, no matter what you did to him he kept coming back for more? The fact that he kept coming back for more abuse, did that make your heart grow fonder for him, or, did it make you lose total respect for him?

Now, let me ask, if you can't stand or respect a man because he lets you treat him like shit, then why would you expect a man's heart to grow fonder or respect you when you let him treat you like shit?

In other words, the same way you feel about a man who lets you shit on him, is the same way he feels about and sees you. Get it?

I GOT SOMETHING OUT OF THE TINA EXPERIENCE

The Tina scenario wasn't all for nothing. I learned something about myself. Sure it didn't work out with Tina, but it did awaken something inside of me that made me view women and myself differently. I realized that I liked being good to a woman. I liked going through my day and having someone to think about. I liked the idea of wanting to be there and take care of somebody. It was a nice feeling. *Yes, I think I want to be a better man, and yes, I want to change my ways. And I will!*

For the first time in my life, when it came to women I was evolving. But, I was in for a surprise.

63

WOMEN LIE, THEY DON'T WANT TO BE TREATED GOOD?

I started a new chapter in my life of treating women right. I treated them like a person, a human being with feelings, thoughts and emotions. I was romantic, caring and sincere. I listened to their every word, even did the little things. I became that good man that all women claimed to want. But, the more I became that man to these females, the more I found myself being pushed away or put in the, "Friend zone." I might as well have had the plague. Women were avoiding me something awful.

When I was a player, I was having sex with up to two girls a day when I wanted to. Women wanted me. My phone rang at all hours of the night to where I would have to disconnect it. But, when I became the, "Nice guy," all of a sudden I found myself staring at my phone in silence?

I was no longer appealing to these women. I was "Nice" to them, but I wasn't a pushover. I was good to them, but I wasn't a doormat. I was there for them, but I wasn't their girlfriend. Still, they didn't want me. All of a sudden women who I would typically run game on and have them crying and banging on my door at 2 A.M. were now rejecting me? This confused me. I didn't want to go back to my old player ways, but what part of the game was this? In retrospect it was so obvious what was going on. To them I was a nice guy, these women didn't want that. To them, nice guys weren't "Dangerous, exciting, out the box, sexy" or "take charge" types of guys. Instead, women viewed them as "Safe, boring, predictable," to these women there was nothing attractive about that. But at that time I couldn't see it. In my mind I was the same person I was before. I just wasn't the asshole that I used to be.

Before writing this chapter I even wrote down all of the women I've pursued who rejected me while I was a great guy to them. I counted twenty-four women. Twenty-four different women whom I was genuinely attracted to and interested in, but after courting and dating them as the nice guy, all of them rejected me. The twenty-four women on this list were different races, ages, backgrounds and had different careers and interests. However, the one thing that they all had in common was they didn't respond to me when I was, "Textbook nice" to them.

HEATHER

Heather was a beautiful woman in the past who I was courting. She always stood out to me. After making a sincere effort to win her affections by being the, "Nice guy," she continuously shot me down. She did think that I was a great friend. I stopped pursuing her and we lost touch with each other. Four years later we ran into each other and became "friends" again. I say "friends" with a, I didn't care one way or the other attitude.

She was also married. I would learn from her friend that her husband was physically and verbally abusing her. I asked Heather about this one day and she confirmed it. I asked her the obvious question as to why she doesn't leave him, she responded, "Because I love him."

The following months when we would talk she would always tell me stories about all the great things she's doing for her husband like buying him gifts and helping him with projects. She was so happy and proud that she was assisting and doing for her, "hands-on," husband. Still, the beatings continued.

One day while talking to her, I said: "You just need to leave this guy, he's too immature and he's beating the crap out of you daily, just leave!" She shouted back, "Oh, you're just mad and jealous because you know you still want me. Don't be petty because I kicked you to the curb. I love him and I'm not leaving him!"

Instead of shouting back at her, I was calm in my response; I said, "You kicked me to the curb? You had a man who treated you like a queen and thought the world of you and you rejected me and chose a man who beats the shit out of you every day, and you think that makes me look bad. No, Heather, I don't want you, actually I feel sorry for you." We never spoke again.

YES, MOST GUYS THINK YOU WANT THIS

What men see from their perspective is women secretly want the bad boy, hard-ass, shit talker, cocky, arrogant, treat women like shit guy. Even if it's not true, this is what the majority of guys believe, because no, women don't say they want this type of guy with their words, but with how they respond to a guy's bad attitude and negative behavior.

A guy treats you like crap not only because he's emotionally uninvolved or you're letting him, but because he thinks this is what you must like. After all, you keep coming back for more, right? So he can only conclude that there must be something about him treating you like shit that you find appealing, yet he doesn't know exactly what it is. I think pancakes mixed with anchovies and onions sounds gross, but if I fed it to you every day and I saw that you kept eating it and coming back for more, than I can only conclude that you must like it, right? However, when I try to feed you the nice steak and lobster dinner (nice guy), you keep pushing the plate away and rejecting it.

Now, as adults, we know and understand that women don't like this abusive type of behavior from a man. Also, most women who do respond to men like this have deep, psychological, low self-esteem and daddy issues or whatever her cliché is, but guess what, the thing is, men aren't reading into it that deep. Guys don't care about your past or life issues, or about what makes you repeatedly come back for more abuse after you didn't get the clue the first time. Some guys know one thing, "Treat'em like shit, and they'll always come back for more," because they've seen that this gets results. Of course, I'm not suggesting that men who are good to women should start treating them like crap. But, it's more of a question of what's going on inside of you that you would continuously let a man treat you like crap and keep coming back for more? I tell women all the time who are being physically and emotionally abused by men that, "You don't have a man problem, but a self-esteem problem."

64

I CAN CHANGE HER

Are you the type of woman who likes to party, sleeps with a lot of different guys and is considered a little easy? Maybe you like to drink and get shit faced on the weekends and do your drug of choice. In other words, you're a little wild and out there and you're doing your share of dirt.

While all of this is going on you have this one guy in your life that continuously tries to win you over, tries to make you his woman and wants to be in a relationship with you. Maybe you have a hard time figuring out what this guy sees in you knowing that he knows about your wild ways and that you don't seem to be slowing down anytime soon. Plus you keep waving a big red flag and show no real romantic interest in him whatsoever. Sure he's a nice guy, but he just doesn't do it for you, but he's still trying to win your affections.

OK, NOT THAT I CARE, BUT WHY DOES HE WANT ME?

He's made up his mind that you're who he wants. He's already fallen in love with you and now he's just working on sealing the deal. First he's attracted to you physically. More than likely, to him, you have a beautiful or pretty face. Some guys can see a pretty face on a woman and can't get past that. Once your beauty smites a guy he begins to see everything else about you as beautiful. That part of his brain that recognizes all of your negative characteristics is disabled, and the part of his brain that only recognizes your excellent qualities heightens. In other words, he'll only see the good in you, even when you're disregarding him. Sometimes you can push him away and kick him out of your life and he'll leave, but, he'll continue to think about you and be concerned with how you're doing. And after enough time has passed he'll make contact to see what's new and going on in your life.

You might think that this type of behavior is coming from a pathetic man with no backbone, but it's the opposite, he has a strong backbone, that's why he's still standing his ground and fighting for you, even in the face of adversity and rejection. He knows that you're sleeping around and dating other guys, but he's still going to let it all play out with the belief that one day you're going to come to your senses and he'll be there waiting for you with open arms. Sound familiar?

Somewhere along the way we let society teach us that someone being eager about us is a bad thing. Think about that for a minute. We've conditioned ourselves to accept that if someone continues to treat us like shit, that behavior is still normal, you don't like it, but you're used to it, it's familiar. But, if someone is really into us and has no problem showing us how much they like us with lots of attention, then their behavior is weird, and they have to be pushed away, fast. You'll fight to hold onto the man who doesn't honestly want you, but quickly dismiss the guy who's willing to sacrifice and pay his dues to be with you?

Knowing what I know now, those women who were eager for me in the past, no way in hell would I push them away? In fact, I'd embrace the eagerness. But, the ones I thought had more value because, "They were a challenge," today, I wouldn't give them a second glance.

HE'LL SEE THINGS IN YOU THAT AREN'T EVEN THERE, AT LEAST ON THE SURFACE

He doesn't want to think anything negative about you so he'll begin to manifest positive qualities in you that don't even exist. All guys that are or have been smitten by a woman's beauty are guilty of this. You might be thinking, *Well, then his love for me can't be real, because now you're saying that he sees things in me that aren't even there?* No, that doesn't mean that he doesn't see the real you; it means the opposite, he does see the real you, but, he wants to hold onto that image of the real you so badly that he doesn't want any negative thoughts about you to alter them. So he adds a little more positive wonderful thoughts and ideas about you to the ones that already exist. Remember, the real you is a woman who is caring, loving, sincere and a child of God. Every man knows that's who all women are on the inside, regardless of all of the dirt you might be presently doing on the outside. He just wants to focus and bring that side out of you more.

While in the courting phase, in his mind, he's getting to know you as a friend and individual. If he hasn't already run for the hills, it just means that so far he likes what he sees about you internally and his fondness for you is growing with each passing day.

LIKE THE CHAPTER TITLE SAYS, "I CAN CHANGE HER"

What does it mean when he thinks that, *I can change her?* It doesn't mean that he wants to control you or change who you are at all. It means that he wants to win you over and kill you with kindness. He feels that if he continuously shows you love, attention, being non-judgmental, being there for you as a friend and giving you a shoulder to cry on even if it's about guy troubles, that eventually you'll come around and appreciate him more. He wants to believe that eventually you'll begin to appreciate him to the point where you'll want to give up your wild partying sleeping around ways and want to give your body and mind to him only. He's not stupid, and he understands that you're wild, but he feels that all you need from him is a little TLC. So he's going to do his best to give that to you as much as he can.

THIS GUY IS YOUR REAL PRINCE CHARMING

This particular guy that I'm talking about is the greatest guy that you're ever going to meet. Because in his mind you're the only woman in the world that exist. When it comes to you, his true intentions are to rescue you, even if you don't think you need rescuing. He wants to be your hero. He's the one who thinks so much of you and wants to be with you regardless of your dirty ways that he's even willing to pay his dues and be patient with you until you finally come around. Unfortunately most women never come around, and after a while he gets the message and moves on, and you end up with one loser after another who takes you for granted instead of choosing the man who was fighting for you.

65

NICE GUYS DON'T FINISH LAST, STUPID FEMALES DO

The last few chapters you've been reading were all leading up to this chapter and to make this point, but it's true, stupid females do finish last, not nice guys. It's a fact!

Nice guys are usually nothing more than just males who have mentally and emotionally evolved faster and earlier than the other males around him. That guy who you perceive as being, "Too nice" and continue to reject or put in the "friend zone" eventually ends up with a woman who can appreciate his good heart and kindness. Because that particular female has figured out that in the end, being with a guy who is good, kind and attentive is what's really important and has real value. She's going to reap the benefits of the, "nice guy" and get the loving husband, great house, great kids, etc, because she had enough common sense to figure out that, "nice" equals blessings and progress.

But then you have the females who still haven't figured this out and are still placing value in guys who are assholes, immature, and are physically and verbally abusive, in other words, the "Bad boy?" But, the woman who is continuously drawn to the "Bad boy," because she's convinced herself that there is some value or sex appeal in this type of behavior, in the end, usually ends up holding a bag full of shit. In other words, nothing.

I can think of about forty females I know who've rejected the nice guys and have chased the "Bad boys" for years. And out of the forty women do you know how many of them are actually in positive relationships today? Three. With nice guys, of course. But those odds are terrifying. Three have figured it out, but the rest are still stuck on stupid. What's kind of sad is the ones who haven't figured it out are now struggling to pay their bills and raising their kids that they had with their "Bad boy" and getting no help from these men. Some have three or four baby's daddy's and still can't get help. Most of these, "Bad boys" turned out to be losers in the end. Looks like somebody bet on the wrong horse.

I'm telling you right here and now as a guy, "Bad boys" are nothing more than males who just haven't figured it out yet, again, grown little boys who haven't evolved emotionally.

What's also sad about this is how females follow these idiots off of cliffs. You're following someone because you think he's "Cool, great" or "Has it together, swag." When in reality he's just as lost and clueless as you are. But, you're so blind to that fact because you're too busy seeing things in him that aren't there.

Yes, you should feel very stupid and foolish. As long as you continue to entertain him you deserve to be heartbroken, cheated on, treated like crap and abused. What's the matter? Are you mad at me for what I just said? You think I'm wrong? If I'm so wrong then why are you still with him? Why are you still thinking about him? Why are you still crying over him? Why haven't you walked away from him by now? I'll tell you why, "Because I still love him. I'm hoping he'll change. He'll appreciate me more after I have his baby. He's just under a lot of stress. I have no self-esteem so this is all that I think I'm worth." Very sad.

I'LL SETTLE DOWN WITH A NICE GUY
AFTER THE SMOKE CLEARS

Some women think that they're just going to use the nice guy as their safety net. In other words, when their done being wild or have let enough, "Bad boys" run up inside of them they'll settle down with a "nice guy" and live a comfortable life. The problem with that mentality is you should only marry for love and that the other person completes you. Not because you're trying to convince yourself that marrying a, "Nice guy" gives you the financial stability you want. It's a house of cards waiting to fall.

I have a friend, Laura, who was a "Bad boy" chaser, but years later she married a "nice guy." Their marriage lasted only two years. She said that in the end she discovered that she wasn't in love with him, but she just wanted the financial security that he could offer. I know her ex-husband, and he is a great guy. He is entirely husband and marriage material. Her problem is, even at her age she still hasn't figured out what's important and what type of a man has real value. She's still chasing the illusion. She still wants the guys from her past and none of them were, "nice guys." To this very day, she is still single. But, in her defense, she still gets to have bad boys with benefits rotating in and out of her bed every week. How fulfilling.

I have another friend, Kim, who's forty-seven, and for years I've been trying to tell her to leave those simple-minded dumbasses alone and start talking to men who have it together, "A nice guy." To this very day she's still on social sites complaining about how she can't find a good man and how come the man she met who's in prison won't write her anymore? Very sad. She has self-esteem issues, and the concept of being treated nice and like a human being is lost on her.

LET'S BE HONEST. WHAT IS THIS REALLY ABOUT? SEX APPEAL!

When it comes to men, many women place a man's value in what they consider to be sex appeal. Sex appeal in a man can come in all shapes and sizes. From his body, face, cologne, confidence and even sense of humor, and of course money! Among other things. We all know that women's brains release certain chemicals when around a particular guy with a kind of Neanderthal behavior.

In most cases, to a woman, the nice guy doesn't represent sex appeal, danger or excitement, which doesn't equal sexual turn on or extra sauce on the taco. Also, most nice guys don't motivate a woman to go to her panty drawer and take "Harry" out for a walk when she's by herself in bed.

OK, I'll admit, the taco example was a bit too much.

But sex is always better when you're in love, and that means being in love for the right reasons. The truth is, I can't tell you what love or being in love is or should mean to you. But I'll tell you this; it doesn't involve constant pain, crying, uncertainty and being in a relationship with a loss of direction and no foundation.

When you've found someone who wants to take care of you, and I don't just mean financially, you've found love.

When you've found a man who wants to sit by your side to comfort you when you're suffering from a contagious flu, you've found love.

When you've found someone who wakes up early so he can shovel the snow off the driveway and off of your car so you don't have to, you've found love.

When you've found a man who has no problem cleaning up your puke that's all over the living room/bedroom floor and the walls, because you had too much to drink with your girlfriends the night before, you've found love.

Also, when you've found a man who'll get out of bed in the middle of the night to feed and change the baby's diaper so you won't be disturbed and can continue your peaceful sleep, you've found love.

And if that's what comes with being with a nice guy, who could complain?

GOD IS TRYING TO BLESS YOU STUPID!

God will bring a lot of great, "nice guys," into your life, because He loves you and wants to see you, His daughter happy and treated right. But how many times will you continue to reject a nice guy He's trying to bring into your life before He just throws His hands up in the air and says, "If she's not trying to receive the great blessing I'm trying to give her, then I'll have to tie my hands and give this great man to my other daughter Danielle, who lives eight miles away and she'll appreciate him."

Now, Danielle reaps the blessing, benefits and gets treated like a queen by a man that was supposed to be yours. Yes, God takes what was supposed to be your blessing and gives it to another woman because you were too stupid to realize what you had. You squandered your blessing because you thought the wrong types of men had value. You saw value in the, "Bad boy," and the qualities you saw in the "bad boy" gave you the impression that this was appealing and dismissed the, "Nice guy."

You see, a lot of women keep asking God to bring a good man into their lives, but the problem is a lot of women also have preconceived notions and ridiculous ideas about what a good man is and the kind of man they want God to give them. When, in fact, God knows what you need better than you do. He knows you better than you know yourself. He created you and knew you before you were in the womb. But, instead of receiving the great man that God is trying to give to you, you send that great man back to God and tell Him that the man He sent you doesn't fit your ideal or criteria. So you spend the next four to five years in relationships where you're being taken for granted, unappreciated, no affection, crying all the time, arguing, and just flat out being treated like you're his cousin as opposed to his woman, duh, still can't figure it out? And guess what? Remember, Danielle, the woman who lived eight miles away. She's now married to that great, "Nice guy" that was supposed to be yours. They're living in a great home and now have two wonderful children together, and she wouldn't change her life for anything. Too bad, that could have been you.

You see, God will bring something good into your life, even a man, but, He won't make you receive him. Because God giving you a good man and you receiving him are two different things. That's why this chapter is titled, "Nice guys don't finish last, stupid females do."

66

HE WANTS YOU BACK BECAUSE HE SAW YOU WITH ANOTHER MAN. BUT NOT REALLY?

Guys do this all of the time. They drop a woman who they're dating or in a relationship with, but later, when they see her in the arms of another man, lookin all happy, all of a sudden they convince themselves that she looks a hundred times more beautiful and desirable.

IT'S AN EGO THANG

All it means is when he sees you with that other man his ego gets dropped down a few pegs. And the only way he can feel validated again is by putting you back in a position where you make your world revolve around him like it used to. In other words, it's not you that he wants to be with, but it's about the validation he gets of having you when he wants to. He wants to prove that you still love him and prove to himself subconsciously that he can take you away from your new man at any time. Again, it's all about his ego.

So we as men lie to ourselves in two ways.

1. Since we saw you with your new man, we now convince ourselves that we find you more desirable and attractive.
2. Since we saw you with your new man, we now convince ourselves that we're more in love with you than ever before.

Make no mistake, we don't find you more desirable and we're not in love with you more than ever before. We're just going through the jealous motions, that's it. But, let's say for example you do decide to go back to him, once he has you back where he wants you, then that's when you'll see, "Him" return. You'll realize nothing's changed.

It's kind of sad because I've seen women give up some great men to go back to their exes because their exes convinced these women that they want another chance. So these women dropped the great guy that they were dating and went back to "Dumb ass." And by the time they figured out that nothing's changed with him, the great guy that they've dumped moved on with someone else and now the other woman has their great guy and they have nothing. Because they were too stupid to realize that they needed to leave "Dumb ass" in their past and continue with the "great new guy," they ended up fucking themselves over in the end.

IN CLOSING

Also, no, don't be trying to fan the flames by putting specific pictures on your page because you know it'll get a reaction out of your ex either. It's time to move on emotionally. If you're still acknowledging your ex in any way, it only means that you still want him around in your life in some form. In the end you're only fuckin yourself over, and if you do, that's on you.

The more you entertain him, the more he's going to come at you and be a strain on your current relationship. If you got a new man who's treating you better, then you need to hold onto and direct any thoughts of love and admiration toward him and let that blossom into something that you need in your life, real love, not games.

67

IF HE'S REALLY IN LOVE WITH YOU, HE'LL STOP SELLING DRUGS

When a man has fallen in love and has found the woman he wants to spend the rest of his life with, he'll quickly cut out all of his negative activities. Why? His only motive is not to do anything that will separate him from his heart's desire. He won't want to do anything that can get him locked up for five to twenty-five years. He knows if he were locked up, by the time he gets out you would have already moved on with someone else. No way will he chance it if he's in love, because every drug dealer with common sense knows that you either end up in jail or dead, and there's no real future in the business.

The fast and easy money is not that much of a temptation and if he's successful at being a drug dealer then he knows he's got enough money and it's time to tie up loose ends, get out and invest his money into a business or something legitimate so the both of you can start a life together.

WHAT DOES HIM SELLING DRUGS HAVE TO DO WITH HIM BEING IN LOVE WITH ME?

It's psychological, and I'll explain it to you. You have to remember, when a man who's selling drugs finds that special woman or "The one," the only thing on his mind is settling down, starting a family and having a secure home and life together. He'll only want positivity surrounding him because that's how she'll make him feel. He's no longer drawn to negative activities, people or environments. He'll try to find ways to detach himself from those things, why?

Her love will show him that there's another side to life, that there's more to life than the all mighty dollar. I'm not talking about the way things should be, but the way they are.

A man who sells drugs also knows the riff-raff and company that comes along with it and if he were in love with his woman then he wouldn't want her to ever become a victim to a possible drive-by or attempted murder. If he's not giving up his drug-dealing ways it's because you don't motivate his heart or emotions and losing you is not that serious to him. In short, he's not in love with you.

DON'T LET THE MATERIAL GIFTS FOOL YOU. YOU'RE JUST HIS MAIN GIRL

So many women who are dating drug dealers have allowed themselves to be put into the category of just being these guys's "Main girl." What does it mean to have this privilege?

1. It means you may get to live with or marry him.
2. It means he trusts you and you get to know where he hides his drugs and money around the house.
3. It means that he'll confide in you about things like criminal activities and possibly murders and other ventures that he wouldn't tell anybody else.
4. It means he'll trust that if the police or FBI ever questions you about his criminal activities that you'll go to bat for him and deny and admit to nothing.
5. It also means that he'll trust you with the names and info of the other drug dealers and street clientele that he does business with and even have you meet with them from time to time to do an exchange for him.
6. You get to drive his expensive cars if he hasn't already bought you one.
7. You get to spend his money with a carefree attitude.
8. You also get to eat out in nicer restaurants where you don't have to refer to your meal as a number 4 or 6.

THE ONLY LOSER IN THE END IS YOU!

Oh, ye of little expectation, self-esteem and simple mind. I understand to some females that on the surface this may seem appealing, exciting and attractive. To some females it may make them feel chosen from their drug-dealing man that they put on a pedestal and hold in such high regard because "If he has money, that makes him somebody and mysterious," right? The reality is you're just his main girl, and more than likely he has other women on the side. Also, you're in a relationship with a man who's not in love with you.

Let me add that some women are OK with being a drug dealer's main girl and are also OK with being in a loveless relationship as long as their necessary bills are paid. I'm just putting it out there.

For the woman who is deluding herself that she has a good man and a healthy relationship because of the material gifts and the financial stress-free lifestyle, what you're not realizing is that you're in a situation where the only loser in the end will be you. Here are a few reasons why:

REASONS

1. You're not the only female attracted to his persona and money. Chances are he's taken advantage of this attention and screwing other girls.
2. He'll either end up sentenced to five to twenty-five years or dead.
3. You'll end up having his baby and in the end you'll be the one struggling to provide for the child while he's doing five to twenty-five years or dead.
4. You're setting yourself up as an accomplice. The police have been investigating him, built up a case against you as his accomplice and now you're looking at a hefty prison sentence. If the police raid the house where you both live and find drugs or drug paraphernalia, regardless of who they belong to, you can be found just as liable as him. That also includes murders.
5. You can also have your kids taken away from you, permanently!

WALK AWAY!

No man who's in love will put the woman he's in love with in those types of situations or circumstances. No drug dealer with common sense thinks he's too good or too smart to get arrested or even killed while hustling the streets.

Therefore, the bottom line is, if he's still selling drugs, whether small-time or moving a lot of product, while he's supposed to be in a relationship with you, then he's not in love with you. Walk away on your own, or walk away in handcuffs or a stretcher.

68

EXPENSIVE GIFTS AND SECURITY DOESN'T MEAN HE'S IN LOVE WITH YOU

Some women can make the mistake of thinking that just because their man buys them expensive gifts or spends money on them that it means he's in love with them. Not always.

A man who's not in love still buys the woman in his life expensive gifts for two reasons. The first reason is that you're his main girl, and even though he's cheating on you, he still wants to make you happy because he loves you, but not in love with you. So, he has no problem with buying you expensive jewelry, a new car, or taken you on exotic vacations and shopping sprees.

The second reason is to control you. In other words, "Even though I'm not in love with you, you're still my main girl, and I'll still buy you expensive gifts so that way you'll owe me." Did you hear that? So you can owe him. What do I mean by that? From an emotionally immature man's perspective, no matter how much he fucks up or cheats on you or disregards your feelings, as long as he's buying you expensive gifts or taken care of you, you owe him. Therefore, you better not fuck up, cheat on him, or disregard his feelings. If you do fuck him over that makes you a scandalous, gold-digging, ungrateful, don't know what you had, fucked off a good thing, bitch, and every other derogatory name men use to degrade women. That's how men think.

Even in this day and age of relationships men still think with a double standard. The bottom line is security and material things don't always mean he's going to be a good man to you; so many women had to learn this the hard way.

69

JEALOUS, POSSESSIVE, CONTROLLING MEN. RUN FOR THE HILLS!

Run for the hills! Move out of your place and don't leave a forwarding address. Change your number and maybe your job. In some cases move to a different state!

I think that men who are rapists and who hit women are two of the lowest forms of men that there are. But men who are extremely jealous, possessive and controlling are definitely in my top five. I can't stand these weird, insecure guys who want to control a woman, especially to that extreme.

Every year thousands of women are stalked, beaten and killed by these types of men, and they can turn your world and life upside down in a second! Why are some men so jealous, possessive and controlling? Well, there are plenty of reasons. It would be pointless for me to break down the male psyche and way of thinking because it's not even necessary. Seriously, is it essential to know why your neighbor's pit bull attacked and bit you? no it isn't, you just know that it did. After you sue for damages and while your wounds are healing you know never to go near that pit bull again. It's not your job to figure him out; it's your job to get as far away from him as fast as you can! The jealous, possessive and controlling man has serious insecurities and emotional issues that have nothing to do with you, but again, he's going to make his problems your problems, if you let him.

HE SEES ME AS HIS PROPERTY, THAT TURNS ME ON. WHAT'S WRONG WITH THAT?

Some female's self-esteem and self-worth are so low that they see their man's jealousy and possessiveness as a form of attention, love and affection.

OK, I get it. I understand that there are women who like the idea of a man making a fuss over them because it makes them feel wanted, needed and worth fighting over. However, the reality is that's not what's happening here. That's not the kind of reason you want a man to fight for you. A man fights and makes a big fuss over his woman to protect her honor, not to control and abuse her emotionally.

Even if you know you're not being honest with yourself and you still want to buy into the illusion that he's possessive and controlling because he loves you and you like the false validation, that's a decision you'll have to live with and suffer the consequences for what unfolds. I don't know of any relationship that had a happy ending when one or the other parties were jealous, possessive and controlling.

Remember, these men are not in love with you, because they're incapable of being in love with you. Their primary function is to control because that's their comfort level. No real man who's genuinely in love wants to control or manipulate his woman, it just doesn't exist.

Many relationships ended with the woman's body found in a trunk of a car deep in the woods or lake. You think that's too extreme and your man won't go that far? Well guess what? so did most of those women whose bodies were found months after they were killed. Men have even been known to set their women on fire while still alive over jealous behavior.

Jealousy is a son of a bitch! It can make a man do and think some crazy shit. Do you really want to see just how far this idiot will go? There is no hope for this man, he is what he is, and if another woman wants to make it her problem that's between her, him and the local police, because once you get involved with a jealous, possessive, controlling man, the local police becomes part of your relationship — kind of like a silent partner with pepper spray.

You'd be surprised how many restraining orders are issued each year over men who are possessive and controlling. If you're content with the kind of relationship where you have to call the police on him every two months, then he's no longer the problem, you are!

YES, MY MAN IS A LITTLE POSSESSIVE, BUT HE'S NOT THAT BAD

There's no such thing as a little possessive, either he is or he isn't. There's a problem with this way of thinking. What you're not realizing is that his, "little possessiveness," can quickly turn into something much more significant in a matter of seconds under the right circumstance, and gets worse as time goes on. One minute he's just a, "little possessive," and only asking you, "Where have you been?" and "who were you with?" and the next minute he's checking your text messages. He'll question all your phone conversations, check the mileage on your car, drive around to the places that you like to go to like friend's houses/restaurants and clubs. If he doesn't know where you're at he'll call all of your friends to see if you're with them, and if they deny you're with them he'll get angry, start yelling and accusing them of lying. I knew of a guy who was so jealous and possessive that whenever his girlfriend would come home a little late, even if she did nothing wrong, he would make her take off her panties and sniff them to see if she'd been having sex with someone else. Well guess what, I'm sure in the beginning he didn't start out that way, he was just a, "little possessive." She decided to stay with him and entertain his, "little possessiveness" ways and attitude, and now a year later he's sniffing her panties? That's what I mean when I say that his, "little possessiveness," can turn into something much greater!

HE THREATENS TO KILL HIMSELF IF YOU LEAVE HIM OR DON'T TAKE HIM BACK

For the most part, when a guy threatens to kill himself over you, it's usually just a manipulative control tactic. He thinks if he's convinced you of his suicidal tendencies that you'll become overwhelmed with guilt and he'll be on your mind more. He also thinks threatening to take his own life will convince you how much he loves you, "I love you so much that I'll kill myself over you!"

IT DOES HAPPEN

I've had a few associates kill themselves over a woman. Not to sound insensitive, but the truth is, if a guy is threatening to end his life over a woman, including you, he's got more in-depth issues that have nothing to do with you. He needs to get help to deal with the real demons he's battling and stop pretending that you hold the key to whether he continues to live or die. Don't fall for the guilt games, and don't think it's your fault if he follows through. It's OK to let him know you care for him as a person and he needs to get professional help, but you are never going back to him and cutting the cord, meaning cutting off communication. The reason you have to put your foot down and cut the cord in this way is because he might try to prey on your weak vulnerabilities, meaning play the, "You said you were my friend! You said you cared about me!" card. If he needs someone to talk to he's got a million other friends, family members and there are a million churches and suicide hotlines to call.

Bottom line, I hope he never does, but you need to move on with your life.

HE MADE ME CUT FAMILY AND FRIENDS OUT OF MY LIFE

If a man is asking or telling you to cut loved ones out of your life, especially those who aren't offensive or pose any threat to either of you, dump his ass on the spot! Now, I understand that everybody has loved ones who can be toxic. Also, you should put distance between them and you. However, that's not what I'm talking about here. I'm talking about when he tells you to cut loved ones out of your life for his selfish reasons.

The reasons he'll tell you to cut out loved ones is because either they pose a threat to him, like if he knows your concerned aunts, cousins or friends love you and are telling you to leave his abusive ass. Or he'll tell you to cut out guy friends because of his petty jealousy. These guy friends in your life can be like brothers/cousins to you, and he'll still be immature about it.

Unfortunately, I've had women in my life who I've considered to be like family that have cut me off for a controlling man.

Only an immature un-evolved punk tells you to drop your loved ones to satisfy his ego and comfort. Drop his ass!

HE WON'T LET ME GET A JOB

Yes, guys like to be the provider, but at the same time they have no problem with their woman working. After all, the days of women staying at home to only tend to the house while the men go out to work is long gone. The 50's are over! Not only are today's women conquering CEO's and business owners, but lately in our society it seems that in many ways the women are the primary breadwinners in the home. A man should never make a woman feel like the only thing she's good for is making his dinner and folding his laundry.

The bottom line is, when a man insists or stresses that his woman stays home and to let him be the provider of the house, he's not saying that for honorable reasons such as wanting her to take it easy or to make life easier for her. No matter what any man says as to why he doesn't want you to work, the truth is it's a control tactic, nothing more, nothing less. He wants to be able to control you and keep tabs on your whereabouts. In other words, you should be at home tending to the house and not out attracting or spending time around other guys or with a male co-worker. He expects that when he calls you and you're not in the house, then you should either be at the grocery store, paying a bill, dropping the kids off or bringing him his lunch. Either way, he doesn't want you in a work environment where you can mingle with other guys or male co-workers daily.

BY NATURE, WE ALL GET A LITTLE JEALOUS

Yes, this is true, but there is a word called moderation. There's also a concept called putting yourself in check. There's a big difference between being jealous, and being the extremely jealous type. As men, we know if we're the extremely jealous type. We also know that if we want to be in a fulfilling relationship that we need to work on our insecurities before we even step into a relationship.

It's not as if a guy realizes he's a jealous, possessive control freak after he meets you. He knew this was always inside of him from the beginning, long before he ever met you. He also knows that side of him will eventually come out and he's doing his best not to show that side of himself too early on in the relationship. He's just waiting until he has you right where he wants you emotionally, that's when the floodgates open up.

HE THINKS IT'S ALL YOUR FAULT

He's not going to put himself in check or get counseling to deal with his insecurities, why? Because in most cases, possessive men don't even think that there's a problem with their behavior. These men have convinced themselves that it's the women who make them act this way, and if the women were doing what the men asked them to, or tell them to do, then they wouldn't be so jealous, possessive and controlling towards them. You see, it's all your fault your man acts this way, duh? Eventually it'll turn physical and he'll begin striking and beating you.

So let me remind you again, that these men are not in love with you because they're incapable of being in love with you. Their primary function is to control because that's their comfort level. No real man who's truly in love with his woman wants to control or manipulate her, it just doesn't exist. So, if he's showing any signs of being jealous, possessive and controlling, walk away!

LOOK HIM UP ONLINE

You can easily look up any man to see if they have a criminal record of domestic abuse or has/had a restraining order against them from a previous relationship. So many women were surprised by what they found out about their current boyfriend or someone they were considering getting involved with. They saved themselves years of drama and abuse just by taking ten minutes out of their day and going online to investigate their man or potential man and walking away!

70

HE'S VERBALLY ABUSING YOU

If he's continuously abusing you with his mouth then he's not in love with you. A real man in love is using his mouth to praise his woman and lift her up, give her words of support and encouragement. I'm not telling you the way things should be but the way they are.

Of course I'm not saying that every time he opens his mouth to you that rainbows and butterflies are going to come out of it, I'm saying that it would take a lot for a man in love to verbally abuse his heart's desire. A man can't be in love with a woman and be consistently abusing her with his mouth at the same time; it just doesn't exist.

THERE'S A DIFFERENCE BETWEEN ARGUING AND VERBAL ABUSE

I'm not saying that you two as a couple won't have bad days or arguments and disagreements, and yes, you'll even have days where you'll jump down each other's throats. However, there's a big difference between a man arguing with his woman and a man continuously ripping and cutting his woman down with his words. What do I mean? I'll break down as to what qualifies as verbal abuse.

1. While arguing, does he try to demean you with his words?
2. Does he call you a bitch, cunt, ho?
3. Does he say things like, "Fuck you?"
4. Does he threaten you with physical violence?

5. Does he CONSTANTLY try to use something you did in the past as ammunition against you?

6. Is his communication with you more aggressive than calm on a regular day?

7. Does he talk negatively about your family members?

8. Does he say things against you that he already knows are sensitive subjects and matters?

9. Constantly mocking you?

10. Short with you?

11. Always annoyed or acts like you're inconveniencing him?

12. Acts like what you say is stupid?

WALK AWAY!

I have a lot of female friends and associates, who are in relationships where their man is a constant negative, or they'll be getting along just great one week, then the next week he'll be doing one or all of the lines from the above examples. It doesn't matter, because if he's continuously doing any of these examples at any time, he's not in love with you.

You see, these words and aggressive verbal attacks aren't something that men use and say because we're just so mad at you or we just got caught up in the heat of the moment, or you just provoked us and pushed us too far. We say these things because this is how we regard you as a person who doesn't deserve our respect.

Yes, it's human nature to want to get the better of someone and get a reaction out of them when you're arguing or having a disagreement, but that's not what's happening here. What's happening here is, he doesn't just want to get the best of you, he wants to hurt you! He wants to stick the knife in and turn it verbally. No man in love is continually going to come at his woman in this way, so if he is, walk away!

71

HE'S PHYSICALLY ABUSING YOU

This is a no brainer. Look, if your man is putting his hands on you under any circumstance then he's not in love with you, and let me add he never will be, period! It is impossible for a man who's in love to physically abuse the woman he loves.

What you have to understand is a man in love doesn't want any harm to come to his woman whatsoever. Just the idea alone of you being hurt or having to succumb to any harm tears him apart and hurts him to his stomach, because now that you two are connected emotionally, what happens to you, happens to him. It brings him pain and grief to see you in pain of any kind, and the idea of him being the one who causes you the pain is totally out of the question.

If you're with a man who is or who has physically abused you and you refuse to walk away, then he's no longer the problem, you are! Let's take a look at the excuses that females with low self-esteem are willing to accept from their man and themselves.

IT JUST HAPPENED THAT ONE TIME, BUT
IT HASN'T HAPPENED SINCE

In the sitcom, Grace Under Fire, during one episode, she was talking to a woman who was being physically abused by her husband. Being a former victim of domestic abuse herself, Grace jokingly said, "I used to tell people that my husband was cleaning his fist and it accidentally went off."

Yes, she was being funny, but also making a point about how ridiculous some women sound when they continuously make excuses for the abusive men in their lives.

However, the reality is that if he were in love with you it wouldn't have happened at any time. No man accidentally goes off and hits his woman. He hit you because that's the level he sees you on and that's how he regards you. When it happens again, and it'll happen again, each time will be worse than the last. It only goes down from here.

IT WAS IN THE HEAT OF THE MOMENT, BUT HE SAID HE WAS SORRY

You're right, he is sorry, until the next argument. So I guess that means every time he gets caught up in the heat of the moment you can expect an ass beating that comes with a side of apologies?

HE WAS CRYING AND SAID HE WAS SO SORRY AND BEGGED ME FOR ANOTHER CHANCE. I WANT TO BELIEVE HIM AND GIVE HIM ANOTHER CHANCE

All I can say to that is, **ROUND TWO**! Don't forget to stop at the pharmacy to get some alcohol for your lips. Sometimes men can turn on the waterworks faster than a woman. Remember, when a man has fucked up with you or runs the risk of losing you because of his foul actions, we as men can be good at playing the sympathy card and turning on the waterworks. We know that women can be suckers for someone in pain, especially when that someone is the person you love. We have no problem with putting on a show and exploiting your vulnerabilities and soft spots. In the end, his crying is all bullshit! If you stay with him expect another ass beating.

HE'S AWESOME TO ME. BUT HE HIT ME ON TWO DIFFERENT OCCASIONS WHEN HE WAS DRUNK. I FORGAVE HIM THOUGH

I know this guy. He's the great guy who's always good and decent to you until he knocks back a few, then his bad side comes out. Let's say for the sake of argument that your man is really in love with you. One evening he has three beers and as a result his Dr.Jeckell and Mr.Hyde personalities revealed. Once that evil side comes out of him, and his abusive personality is exposed, then he would do everything in his power to make sure that side of him isn't revealed again, and that includes him stopping his drinking.

Let's say for example that there was something inside of red apples that made a man in love beat on his woman, no matter how much he likes red apples he won't eat them again as long as he's in a relationship with her. Because his love for her is so strong he won't take the chance of putting something in his system that'll make him lose control and possibly hurt the woman he loves, which includes red apples, beer or any alcohol. If he hasn't stopped consuming the very thing that can lead up to him possibly hurting you, then he's not in love with you.

I PROVOKED HIM BY PUTTING MY HANDS ON HIM FIRST

If you want to use that as an excuse as to why you won't leave him, then that's your business and problem. Unless you're repeatedly striking him with a baseball bat and he's about to go unconscious, then no man has any business hitting you, period!

The bottom line is, men are much stronger than women, and that's not to say that a woman can't do any real damage to a man, because women can be physically abusive when they want to be. However, if a woman is hitting a man, a real man would walk away from her, or do everything in his power to restrain her until she calms down, especially if he's in love with her, but he won't hit her.

I HAVE NOWHERE ELSE TO GO

I know women who have left and started from ground zero to get away from their abusive men. One woman I know took her two kids and slept in her car for a month because she was that serious about getting away from her abusive husband. The bottom line is, you stay there because you want to, and if you want to continue making excuses as to why you can't leave him then don't expect pity from over here. Pack your shit and walk away!

HE HITS ME BECAUSE HE LOVES ME

Some women believe this. These women need counseling. They have some deep-rooted issues.

HE'S UNDER A LOT OF STRESS

We're all under a lot of stress; whether it's money problems, bills, work, etc. Stress can make a man turn to many things like drinking, drug abuse and even suicide. That's not what's happening here. A man in love doesn't put his hands on his woman because he's under a lot of stress. The reason your man is beating on you is because he wants something or someone to feel the pain that he's feeling. You see, as men we like to punch walls and doors when we're angry, but the problem with that is a wall and a door don't feel pain or have the capability to respond, that's where you come in. He wants to take his aggressions out on you because not only does he want you to feel the pain that he's feeling, but it also makes him feel good, in control and empowered to hear you cry and beg for him to stop. He wants to make himself feel better by beating you down. No real man, who's in love, wants to make himself feel better by beating and releasing his aggression out on the woman he loves, period!

HE'S A GREAT GUY WITH A GOOD HEART. IT'S JUST SOMETIMES HE LOSES CONTROL

You remind yourself of that when the next time you're eating and it hurts to open your mouth and chew your food because that's where he punched you.

IT'S HARD FOR ME TO LEAVE HIM BECAUSE I LOVE HIM

I'm happy for you, and that you love him, but you're obviously not in love with yourself, and neither is he.

IN CLOSING

Remember, Kleenex is for blowing your nose and toilet paper is for wiping your ass! They were never designed to wipe or absorb blood off of your face. So if you find yourself using these items more for cleaning up your bloody face than for personal hygiene, then something is wrong.

If a man ever puts his hands on you one time, walk away. I'm not saying once an abuser always an abuser, I'm saying hit me once shame on you, hit me twice shame on me. I don't care if he becomes a born again Christian, has seen the light and the errors of his abusive ways, that's excellent. You wish him well, move on, and if another woman wants him, then let it become her problem and issues, not yours. If you choose to stay with him then you take on the responsibility for everything you get! At that point it'll be about accountability not finger-pointing, unless you're pointing the finger at yourself.

72

HE MAKES NO REAL EFFORT TO STOP HIS SUBSTANCE ABUSE

Can your man be an addict and still be in love with you? Absolutely. Can your man be an addict and still have a loving functional, healthy relationship with you? Absolutely not. Let me say that off the top it's not always easy for anybody who's battling a substance problem to just quit.

Everybody's substance abuse battles are different, and every addict has varying degrees of addiction. If you're with a man who is currently abusing a substance and he's not making any real effort to put the drugs or bottle down then he's not in love with you. What you have to understand is when a man is in love his perception and perspective changes dramatically. That high or feeling he gets from the substances won't even compare to the high he gets from being in love with you.

He knows that he has a demon that he has to defeat but for his woman and his relationship he'll grab his sword and battle the beast. He knows that they're other things that a man can lose his woman to besides another man and one of them is substance abuse. Therefore, he'll do whatever he has to, to turn his life around.

WHAT'S MORE IMPORTANT, MY WOMAN OR MY DRUGS/DRINKING?

He's not stupid, he knows he has a substance problem, but because he's in love he won't run the risk of losing you or letting his substance problem destroy his relationship, so he'll either stop altogether or check himself into a treatment center to receive the proper help he needs. If he's really in love, he'll feel a sense of shame for his addiction problem, but still, he's an addict, and struggles with it. Remember, being an addict is not the focus, but the focus is what he feels he has to lose if he doesn't do everything in his power to stop, and the answer is you. If he's not willing to take the proper steps to get real help then he doesn't care about losing you.

SOMETIMES YOU HAVE TO GIVE HIM AN ULTIMATUM

Nine times out of ten, a man won't take the initiative to quit. Most addicts are in denial and convince themselves that they are in control, because sometimes it's easier for him to lie to himself than quit. If a man is with a woman who is not giving him an ultimatum then he'll continue to abuse his substance of choice. Therefore, you have to lay down the law.

I'm not saying that it's your job to do his thinking for him, or wipe his nose, but sometimes an ultimatum is just what the doctor ordered, and usually works if he's in love and fears that he might lose you. After you give him an ultimatum and he still makes no effort, then that's your cue to walk away and not let him drag you down to obscurity, because that's where he's heading.

HE'S BEEN TO REHAB FOUR TIMES ALREADY

Well, then go a fifth time. If that doesn't work then go a sixth time. If he's really in love with you he'll keep battling until he gets it right, because his love for you is his motivation. That's the truth.

IF HE TRIES TO GET YOU TO EXPERIMENT WITH DRUGS WITH HIM, WALK AWAY!

No man who's genuinely in love with a woman will try to get her to do drugs with him. What you have to understand is, a man who's an addict already knows he's fucked up his own life, but no matter how screwed up his thinking and mind is he always believes that the woman he's in love with is precious and an angel. He won't ask her to do anything that's going to dilute that image he has of her, that includes making her an addict and bringing her down to his level. He doesn't want to destroy her life and the only person in his life that loves him. One fucked up person in the relationship is enough. If he does try to get her to do drugs with him, then he's not in love with her and he's trying to have his cake and eat it too, meaning that he wants to bring his woman into the fucked up reality that he's already drowning in and he doesn't care how it affects her life. That also includes any illegal activity, theft, money scams, etc.

HE SAYS HE CAN QUIT AT ANY TIME BUT DOESN'T, THEN YOU QUIT

There's no silver lining that you can put on drugs or alcohol abuse, it's all bad. If you're in a relationship with a man who's doing drugs or abusing alcohol and says that he can quit at any time but doesn't, then he's lying to himself. Most importantly he's lying to you. Nobody wants to be an addict or live his or her life being in that condition, and if he really could quit he would, bottom line. He's not quitting because he doesn't want to stop. It doesn't mean he's a bad guy, it just means he's in a place in his life where abusing drugs or alcohol or both is part of his daily function, and he's content with that. If that's his choice, then you need to quit him and move on with your life. If you think that a drug addict or an alcoholic is the best you can do then it's time for some severe self-evaluation.

DON'T LET HIM BE DEPENDENT ON YOU

Most substance abusers are the biggest leeches out there and will attach themselves, become co-dependent on you and make their problems your problems, if you let them. They want to borrow money all the time. They always want to borrow the car or need a ride but won't offer gas money. They never do what you ask them to do or slow to do it. He'll eat all the food in the house but won't ever buy any. He won't offer or help to assist you in your daily life. The list goes on and on, but the moment you allow him to leech off of you and become co-dependent, he'll take all he can get from you, even the shirt off your back, if you let him. Walk away!

73

YOU'RE ALWAYS HAVING TO TALK TO YOUR GIRLFRIENDS ABOUT HIM

If you find yourself sitting up all night on the phone with your girlfriends, pouring out your heart and emotions, trying to figure out why he treats you the way he does and disregards your feelings, then your relationship with him is already over. You can prolong the inevitable all you want, but if you don't get a grip on the reality of your broken relationship and yourself, it's only going to get worse for you.

The result is more tears, headache, heartache, going to sleep every night crying and wearing out your girlfriend's ears with the same old redundant stories about the fucked up things this man keeps doing to you. The fact that your "Relationship," is in this position should reflect to you that it's time to move on, and calling your girlfriends to complain or yak about your man problems that you refuse to get a clue about is just making you look foolish.

Calling your girlfriends to complain about him isn't going to change the fact that he's not in love with you. Pouring your heart out to your girlfriends isn't going to make him treat you better. I'm talking ABC facts here.

IF YOU REFUSE TO WALK AWAY THEN SHUT UP ABOUT HIM

Some women love to play the victim. Their man is giving them every red flag in the book but they refuse to leave the relationship. Listen, you don't have the right to complain about your man who's treating you like crap if you continue to stay with him. Many women want to keep holding on to this type of man, but they also want the convenience and luxury of bitching about him to their girlfriends whenever he fucks up, which seems to be all the time. You know who you are.

MY FRIEND WAS WEARING ME OUT

I had a friend who would call me at least once a month for almost two years to complain about her man. At that point they had been together for ten years. In that time he had continuously beat on her, stole money, cheated, and he even slept with her best friend. No matter what negative things he would do to her she would always say, "I love him and I'm not going to leave him!"

I would always listen to her and give her advice as a guy and as a friend. She loved the fact that I was always an open ear to her and gave her real feedback. After a while she finally began wearing me out with her constant complaining about her man, and she already made it clear that no matter what he does she's not going to leave him. Enough was enough for me; I mean really, how many times can he do the same shit to her repeatedly until she finally gets a clue? So, one night she decided to call me to rant about her man. Before she got two sentences into her conversation I cut her off and said, "Look, I really love you as a friend, and I'll always be there for you. You can call me anytime and talk to me about all of your problems or whatever's on your mind, but, I don't wanna hear anymore shit about your man or the problems you're having with him. You've made it clear that no matter what he does to you you're not gonna leave him. I'm getting tired of hearing the same stories from you over and over again. If you haven't figured it out by now that this guy is no good, then you deserve everything he's doing to you."

Now, either two things were going to come out of me giving her tough love, she was going to snap out of it, thanks to me being so firm with her, or she was going to continue to hold on to, "Her man," and just not come to me with her man problems anymore. Which one do you think she did? Yep, she's still with him.

HE'S FAMILIAR

I have another friend who would call me to complain about her man. I asked her, "If he's so bad, why do you keep taking him back and sleeping with him?" Her response was, "Because he's familiar." That was her reasoning, "he's familiar." She doesn't like the way he's treating her, but she keeps going back because that's her comfort zone. She's beautiful, intelligent with a great job, but hasn't figured out that 1+1=2.

For some women, being treated like shit from a man is all they know. So they keep going around the same mountain or dating the same type of guy and getting the same results. Maybe it's fear of coming out of their comfort zones that keeps some of them in these toxic relationships.

Unfortunately, I had to cut the cord with her too cause I got tired of hearing about the same guy treating her like shit every day.

My point is, how many of you are holding onto "him" because "he's familiar," or you're afraid to come out of your comfort zone?

IF YOU WERE A REAL FRIEND YOU WOULD BE THERE TO LISTEN

Wrong! A real friend tells you once to drop this zero, and if you choose to stay with him then don't call me to complain about him anymore. The truth is that most women are making asses of themselves by continuously calling up their girlfriends to talk about the same man doing the same shit to them repeatedly. If they're too naive to walk away then they deserve everything they get. Sad but true.

74

HE WASN'T LIKE THIS IN THE BEGINNING

I know a lot of women say this about their man, "But he wasn't like this in the beginning! He treated me good and was always attentive." That's fine. I also bet his hair length is slightly shorter or longer since you met him. Or he's bought a new pair of shoes since your first date. He's altered his car, like buying new rims or installed new speakers or just got a tune-up. I'm sure many things in his life have changed since that magical time you two went out on your first date. However, it doesn't matter, because at some point he's made a left turn in your relationship and it's time for you to make a right. So put your foot on the pedal and floor it!

SO, WHAT HAPPENED, WHY HAS HE CHANGED?

The point is does it matter why his behavior and habits have changed since you both started dating and how it got to the point where he's not treating you right like he used to? No, it doesn't. Regardless of what happened between the beginning and the moment he began treating you less than, he's fallen out of love and attraction for you. Like I said before it's not your job to figure him out or to figure out why. The reason is that once he falls out of love and attraction for you he's not coming back to you emotionally. Regardless of how much you want to make it work or hang in there. So wasting your brain cells trying to backtrack the precise moment where you think your relationship had taken a left turn is pointless.

MOVE ON!

Trust me; move on with your life. Don't be delusional and try to hold on to the fact that things between the both of you were awesome once upon a time, and you want to believe that you two can still have it all over again with patience, understanding and counseling. Emotionally he's already gone. Walk away!

75

IT'S NOT THAT EASY TO LEAVE HIM

I can't count how many women I've heard say this. All I can say is, when you're sick and tired of being sick and tired, you'll leave him.

76

LIKE I SAID BEFORE, YOU DON'T HAVE A MAN PROBLEM, BUT A SELF-ESTEEM PROBLEM

Most women I talk to about their toxic relationships think they have a man problem, when in fact they don't, they have a self-esteem problem. You need to ask yourself, *what is wrong with my self-esteem to where I would let some man treat me as less than?* You keep making it about him when in fact it's all about you! Go to counseling, start working on you. **You won't be able to look at men differently until you begin to look at yourself differently.**

The truth is, the faster you begin to work on your self-esteem and build your confidence, without even trying, you'll begin to dismiss all the negative things from your life, including men who ain't shit!

77

DON'T EVER GIVE YOUR LOVE TO HIM, BUT SHARE YOUR LOVE WITH HIM

No man, and I mean no man has the power to bring you down or make you feel less than, unless you give him that power over you. He just can't take it.

The problem with you is you keep trying to **give** yourself to a man. You have to stop doing that. You only want to **share** yourself with a man, not **give** yourself to him. You only want to **share** your love with a man, not **give** it to him.

There are so many love songs where a woman vocalist says, "I Give You My Love," or one of Whitney's biggest hits, "Saving All My Love, (For You.)" This is the mindset that gets you women into trouble when it comes to men, because you don't want to give him nothing! Instead, you want to share with him. Share your love, dreams, emotions, and thoughts. So the moment he begins to treat you as less than, takes you for granted and becomes abusive, emotionally, verbally or physically, that love is still yours to take back and share with someone else who'll love and appreciate you.

Remember, share your love with him, don't give your love to him.

78

OK, MR. KNOWS IT ALL. HE MIGHT NOT DO ALL OF THE THINGS THAT YOU TALK ABOUT. BUT I KNOW THAT MY MAN'S STILL IN LOVE WITH ME

Sorry, but if he's not doing the positive things but doing the negative things that I address and talk about in this book, then he's not in love with you. Your man isn't special and no exception to the rules.

What I have learned throughout my years of giving women council and advice is that some women love to argue and defend their man's unappreciative behavior towards them. I would sometimes find myself being sucked into these back and forth arguments.

I would try to explain to certain women that because of the way their men treat them that they're not in love with them and they should walk away. But my advice would fall on deaf ears. That's perfectly fine because they're the ones in the relationship with them, which means they take on the consequences.

Many of these women are so caught up in their pride, vanity and not wanting to accept that their man isn't in love with them that they'll make up every excuse under the sun for their men and relationships. That's perfectly understandable and a natural reaction, but it doesn't change the facts. Making excuses for your man only hurts you in the end. Now, when a woman wants to argue or disagree with me, I say with a smile, 'You don't have to take my word for it. He's your man and your problem, I'm just the messenger, and good luck.'

Even as you read this book, I'm sure I've touched a nerve on specific subjects, and you've disagreed and challenged what I've said. I can honestly tell you without ego or arrogance that I'm right. Why? Because I'm a man and you're a woman, and you can't tell me how a man thinks no more than you can tell me how a skunk thinks.

There's a reason why you're reading this book, the reason is because you wanted to learn about men and their foul ways. That's why I wrote this book and you should absorb as much of it as you can because they're only a handful of men out there that'll sincerely give women this kind of information. So take advantage of this opportunity and use this information as a measure in your relationship with your man.

79

BUT HOW CAN I CHANGE HIM AND MAKE HIM FALL IN LOVE WITH ME?

Before I began writing this book, I spoke to women and asked them what questions they would like to know about their man or men in general. I was shocked to find out that most of the females that I spoke with, who were unhappy about their man's unappreciative behavior towards them, weren't considering getting rid of him or walking away. However, they were more interested in finding answers on how to change the thinking of their unappreciative men. The answer is nothing; there's nothing you can do to change him. If he wanted to be a good man and be in a committed fulfilling relationship with you he would be that's the bottom line.

Women often make the mistake of thinking that there's something they can do to change their man and make their man want to be closer to them emotionally. Nothing can be further from the truth. You can change your appearance with makeup and try a new hairstyle; you can wear more appealing clothes. You can adopt a new personality or try to be something you're not. You can even have his back when he's going through a tough time in his life. You can also go out and buy all of the self-help books on relationships and how to win a man's heart, but you're just wasting your time, because it all means very little. It has nothing to do with your actions or how you support him in different areas of his life. It doesn't matter how good you are to him or how good you are as a person. You could be the best thing that ever came into his life and it still doesn't matter, because either he wants to be with you or he doesn't. Either he's going to show it, or he's not, period!

STOP WAITING FOR VALIDATION

I use this example a lot and I'll say it again. But waiting for some man to validate you is like getting into an elevator by yourself, and hoping that someone else walks in and pushes the number of the floor that you want to go. In other words, you're leaving it in someone else's hands to decide how high you can go.

It's only up to you to decide whether or not you want to go down to the basement where it's cold and dark or if you want to go up to the penthouse suite where you'll have soft music and rose petals leading up to a nice bubble bath that's waiting for you.

STOP FIGHTING FOR SOMEONE WHO ISN'T FIGHTING FOR YOU

Remember, if you find yourself in a position where you have to come up with ways to change him and hold on to him, then not only is he not in love with you, but he was never yours to begin with. As a woman, you should feel ridiculous fighting for someone who isn't fighting for you. Walk away!

80

IN THE END, THE ONLY THING THAT'S GOING TO MATTER IS HOW HE TREATS YOU

It's not about how he looks, how big his dick is, what kind of car he drives, how much money he makes, if your family and friends like him, if he has sexy abs, etc. None of these things matter because they're not deciding factors on whether or not a man is going to treat you like the queen you are.

If he's really in love with you he's going to show it, period! He'll do it by the guidelines I've shown you in this book. These are not just my opinions or beliefs, but how men think overall.

This book wasn't designed to discourage you, but to help you see the man/men in your life differently. Also, to help you see your self-worth in a new way, how you've been settling and how you've seen things in him that aren't even there.

When you finally meet the right guy, no, he won't be perfect, and he'll stumble a little bit along the way. But no matter how the journey may go in your relationship, he always has you and the best interest of your relationship in his heart. When you find a man who's really in love with you, the relationship is easy, not complicated. Even your arguments and disagreements will seem petty compared to the love you share and give each other. If you can't understand why this man is so in love with you, it's because he sees things in you that you sometimes can't even see in yourself. He likes what he sees and wants you. Are you going to close the door or come out of your little box and comfort zone and give love a chance?

For questions or comments to the author, email to walkawaynow@yahoo.com

Printed in the United States
by Baker & Taylor Publisher Services